The E-Business Revolution & The New Economy

E-Conomics after the Dot-Com Crash

F. Gerard Adams
Northeastern University

THOMSON
™
SOUTH-WESTERN

Australia · Canada · Mexico · Singapore · Spain · United Kingdom · United States

THOMSON

SOUTH-WESTERN

The E-Business Revolution & the New Economy
E-Conomics after the Dot-Com Crash
F. Gerard Adams

**Vice President/
Editorial Director:**
Jack Calhoun

**Vice President/
Editor-in-Chief:**
Dave Shaut

Acquisition Editor:
Steve Momper

**Channel Manager,
Retail:**
Chris McNamee

**Channel Manager,
Professional:**
Mark Linton

Production Editor:
Todd McCoy

Production Manager:
Tricia Matthews Boies

**Manufacturing
Coordinator:**
Charlene Taylor

Compositor:
Edgewater Editorial
Services

Editorial Associate:
Michael Jeffers

Production Associate:
Barbara Evans

Printer:
Phoenix Book
Technology

**Sr. Design Project
Manager:**
Michelle Kunkler

Cover Designer:
Beckmeyer Design
Cincinnati, OH

Cover Image:
© Eye Wire

Contents

About the Author

F. GERARD ADAMS is McDonald Professor in the College of Business Administration at Northeastern University in Boston.

After receiving his Ph.D. from the University of Michigan in 1956, he was a business economist in the petroleum industry and served in government at the Council of Economic Advisors in Washington and at the Organization for Economic Cooperation and Development in Paris. He spent the following 36 years at the University of Pennsylvania, where he was professor of economics. In addition to his teaching he was active in business consulting and forecasting.

A man of wide-ranging interests, Professor Adams is primarily concerned with empirical applications of economics. He has worked on a broad range of studies, including models of nations, regions, commodity markets, energy, industries, and firms and the linkages between these models. In recent years, he has been concerned with the economics of development and technical change, particularly the implications of the e-business revolution.

Professor Adams is author or editor of numerous articles and a number of books, among them *Industrial Policies for Growth and Competitiveness, Modeling the Regional Economy, Export Instability and Economic Growth, Stabilizing World Commodity Markets, The Business Forecasting Revolution, The Macroeconomic Dimensions of Arms Reduction, Economic Activity, Trade, and Industry in the US-Japan-World Economy,* and *East Asian Development: Will the East Asian Growth Miracle Survive.*

Preface

It will be news to no one that the economy has been changing rapidly. The idea that there is a "new" economy is being promoted widely. Yet few people seem to know clearly what the notion means, how much or how little empirical support there is for it, and what it is likely to imply for business and the economy.

Despite the dot-com crash, there can be no doubt either about the continued rapid rate of technical change, which is affecting not only the quality of hardware and software (IT: information technology) but also their applications in e-business. There remain critical questions about how the new technologies are being implemented in the world of e-business and how they affect the old bricks-and-mortar economy. There is much discussion but little information about the effects of these changes today and the likely future effects.

This project grew from a series of lectures to executive M.B.A. students at Northeastern University in Boston and from extensive discussions in the United States and abroad with businesspeople and academic colleagues about the e-business revolution and its implications for the world economy. Since so many information and telecommunication technology firms have crashed, it is important to take stock:

- Is the e-business revolution really creating a new economy?

- What are the characteristics of e-businesses, not just the ones that have succeeded but also the ones that failed spectacularly?

- What does economic thinking tell us about the advantages that networked communication and computerized automation offer to the economy?

- Are there still possibilities ahead for renewed rapid growth driven by the technological promise of computers and networks?

- What are the implications of any such possibilities for the U.S. economy and for economies in other parts of the world?

The material in this book is addressed to several audiences:

- *A general professional business audience of those concerned with the question of e-business and the new economy.* These are educated people who wish to inform themselves about what is going on in the business world. Is it really a different world from what it was? In what particulars? How do the differences relate to the effect of the Internet on business and on the aggregate economy?

- *An audience of business managers who face the problems brought about by rapidly changing technology and sophisticated competition.* How can their business operations be adapted to this 21st century world? How much must they invest in hardware and software to participate in the e-business world? What parts of their businesses can gain from computerization and what parts call for good old-fashioned personal contacts? How can new e-business enterprises be created and financed in today's post-crash environment?

- *An academic audience in courses taught at universities. In some cases the materials may be the basis for a course in e-commerce, a subject that is being widely introduced in business schools.* Or they may supplement other business school courses at the M.B.A. or advanced undergraduate levels. Note that the emphasis on economic theory and its implications makes these materials suitable for use in economics courses as well as in more business-oriented courses.

While the present situation of many dot-coms looks grim, especially in the high-tech heartland of Silicon Valley, technological change is irreversible and progressive—a new idea leads to another and those that pay off will be adopted widely. It takes time and effort for new developments to find their way to improvements in economic performance. I am confident that they will.

I would like to thank my son, Mark, himself a dot-com entrepreneur, for his advice on this project.

F. Gerard Adams
February 18, 2003

Part I
The New Economy and the Dot-com Crash

Chapter 1
A New Economy?

In the past decade, the economy and financial markets of the United States have been highly volatile. The extended expansion in the 1990s was interrupted by the collapse of many new dot-com enterprises, a financial crash, and a broad economic recession. Financial markets, particularly those relating to high tech and e-businesses, have taken a significant tumble, reflecting an excessive level of optimism in the 1990s and a probably undue level of pessimism more recently. There remains considerable uncertainty about the economic future of the United States, and indeed of the world. Everywhere the question arises, Does the future hold rapid economic recovery and a return to sustained knowledge-based growth?

There is no doubt that information technology (IT) and e-business are bringing overwhelming changes to the structure and operation of the world of business, but there is obviously some doubt about how that will play out. Many experts have argued that we are living in a new economy, one that will bring renewed growth to our living standards, will ease inflationary pressures, and (or so we thought not very long ago) might even eliminate the business cycle. E-business is the watchword of this new economy.

There is still plenty of controversy about the new economy. Until the recent crash, the statistics of economic performance—growth, productivity, inflation—looked very good, but they remain inconclusive in many respects. The concentration should be not so much on current business cycle statistics as on a longer perspective.

In the United States, we used to accept the notion that ours was a mature economy, one that was destined to grow only very slowly because it had exhausted its potential. No more! We see the U.S. economy as rejuvenated, a leader in technological and managerial growth. Even after a recession and the collapse of so many dot-com firms, we are confident that the evolution of IT—specifically the interconnection of computers to the Internet, the vastly reduced

3

cost of computation and communication, and the application of sophisticated computer programs for business operation and control—will pay important growth dividends.

The IT/E-business revolution, like the industrial revolutions of the 18th, 19th, and early 20th centuries, promises to transform the economy. Admittedly, though, some observers are not so sanguine. Observing the shambles in financial markets, they raise the possibility that the experience of the United States in 1995-2002 was simply another round of the business cycle.

What makes the e-business revolution different from past technology booms? It is not just the rapid productivity gains in the fabrication of chips and electronic equipment, though these play a crucial role. It is not simply, as in past technical revolutions, that machines are replacing muscle power. Instead, high technology is replacing human communication and *brainpower.* Many activities that used to call for human interaction, on paper or over the phone, are now carried out over long distances, automatically or by the click of a mouse on the computer. Our personal as well as work lives have been affected; we communicate by e-mail, order books and other merchandise on the Web, or trade stocks on our computer accounts.

For the business world, too, this is not just a matter of another new technology. Rapid technical change is having a profound influence on how we organize and conduct business. The networked interconnection of millions of computers in the hands of consumers, businesses, and even government is producing an altogether different business environment. The most important changes are in the mechanics of business transactions in both business-to-consumers (B2C) and business-to-business (B2B). The improvements in communication and transportation are transforming international trade and finance. We are on the threshold of fundamental changes in business organization, financing, and location.

Exactly what the changes will mean for the economy is still to be seen. The boom has been rudely interrupted by recession. But perhaps we can be optimistic after all; in the longer term, there should be renewed payoff in terms of faster economic progress.

Is there really an e-business revolution, one that will transform the economy? What kind of revolution is it? How has it affected business? What has been the e-business experience: success or failure? What economic theory underlies it? What are the implications of e-business for the new economy? How will the world economy be changed? These are the concerns of this book.

We have divided our discussion into four parts:

1. We introduce the new economy. What do we see in the performance of the economy that makes it look like a new era? What technological

changes are under way? How do they relate to the organization and performance of the economy? In sum, is there really a new economy?

2. We consider e-business. What are the many possibilities for carrying on business activity on the Internet? How have e-businesses been organized? We present studies of actual experiences, good and bad. What lessons do these case studies suggest for the conduct of e-business? What do they imply for the organization of business? What possibilities do they suggest for the role of new e-business ventures and for the renewal of "old" economy firms?

3. We will look at the economic theory supporting e-business. In what way is it different from traditional economic theory? What are the implications at the level of the enterprise, old and new? How will performance of the aggregate economy be affected? What are the implications for competition and growth?

4. Finally, we look to the future—one that has many uncertainties but offers much potential. Will the recent rapid gains in productivity continue? How long can the knowledge economy continue to expand? What are the international consequences? Who will be the winners? Who will be the losers?

WHAT IS THE NEW ECONOMY?

Is there a new economy? What is it?

Opinions about the new economy range all over the map. Though many economists have argued that we are in a new economy, one that has different characteristics and potential from the old, the strength of conviction about the new economy and its implications varies greatly.

On one extreme are the new economy true believers. They see an altogether new economic world. It's a Goldilocks economy, a dream world where everything is "just right." There is high productivity growth, low unemployment, *and* low inflation. Some for a time even argued that the business cycle was dead, that there would no longer be serious booms and busts.

At the other extreme are the absolute non-believers. They say that the new economy is just like the old. They argue that the productivity growth of recent years is the result of rapid economic expansion and a stock market boom, or, paradoxically, that it is a statistical mirage related to the way technological improvements in computer equipment have been treated in our national income and product statistics.

In between are the majority of economists and business managers. They welcome rapid economic change but recognize that conventional economic principles still apply widely.

The description of the new economy from the *Encyclopedia of the New Economy* makes many important points. It leans toward the optimistic side of this perspective:

> *"So what is a new economy? When we talk about a new economy, we're talking about a world in which people work with their brains instead of their hands, a world in which communications technology creates global competition—not just for running shoes and laptop computers but also for bank loans and other services that can't be packed into a crate and shipped. A world in which innovation is more important than mass production. A world in which investment buys new concepts or the means to create them, rather than new machines. A world in which rapid change is a constant. A world at least as different from what came before as the industrial age from its agricultural predecessor. A world so different its emergence can only be described as a revolution."*[1]

Many dimensions of the operations of the economy are involved. The *Encyclopedia of the New Economy* provides lively definitions for many terms connected with the new Economy, ranging from A—*adhocracy* (whatever that may mean) to Z—zero sum.[2]

Views on the new economy are closely linked to improvements in the performance of the economy, yet the 2001 recession did not wipe out all optimism. This is apparent from what influential people have been saying (Table 1.1).

Mike Mandel, a journalist at *Business Week,* like many other experts emphasizes the accelerated rate of productivity growth that we have witnessed in the last few years.

Larry Summers, then Secretary of the Treasury and now president of Harvard University, reminds us that the bases of the new economy are the same as that of the old: thrift, investment, and market forces. Indeed, the operation of entrepreneurial markets is one of the underpinnings of the new economy. On the other hand, Robert Gordon from Northwestern University takes a more pessimistic view, questioning whether the new economy measures up to the great inventions of the past.

---

[1]John Browning and Spencer Reiss. "Introduction."*Encyclopedia of the New Economy,* Lycos. <*http://hotwired.lycos.com/special/ene*>.
[2]<*http://hotwired.lycos.com/special/ene*>.

Table 1.1 What People Have Been Saying

- Mandel (*Business Week*)
  –A key characteristic of the New Economy . . . is an accelerated rate of productivity growth (November 2000).
- Summers (Treasury)
  –The New Economy is built on old virtues: thrift, investment, and letting market forces operate. (January 2003)
- Gordon (Northwestern)
  –Does the New Economy Measure up to the Great Inventions of the Past? (Fall 2000)
- Economic Report (Council of Economic Advisers)
  –The current situation . . . reveals no obvious signs of an imminent slowdown. . . . The most likely prognosis [is] sustained job creation and continued non-inflationary growth (February 2000).
- Greenspan (Federal Reserve)
  –Irrational exuberance (December 1996).
  –A set of imbalances that . . . threaten our continuing prosperity (February 2000).
  –An infectious greed seemed to grip the business community (July 2002).
  –The fundamentals are in place for a return to sustained healthy growth (July 2002).
- Meyer (Federal Reserve)
  –The global slowdown stems principally . . . from the sharp slowdown under way in the United States (May 2001).
- Federal Open Markets Committee (Federal Reserve)
  –For the longer term, prospects for rapid technological progress and associated faster productivity growth are scarcely diminished (October 2001).

Just before the recession in 2000, the Council of Economic Advisers in Washington saw nothing ahead but jobs and non-inflationary growth, a forecast that may have been excessively optimistic about short-run macroeconomic prospects.

There were clearly some risks in excessively rapid expansion, particularly inflation of stock prices. Alan Greenspan, chairman of the Federal Reserve, was already talking about *irrational exuberance* back in 1996 when the Dow index was at 6,500. In 2000, when the Dow was close to its peak at 11,000, he reminded us again that serious imbalances in the economy threatened continued prosperity.

The optimistic perspectives on the new economy were called into question abruptly early in 2001 by the dot-com crash and the recession. Yet while Federal Reserve Board member Laurence Meyer warned of a global slowdown starting with the recession in the United States, the Fed's Open Market Committee felt that prospects for faster productivity growth were hardly diminished—a sentiment that was echoed by Chairman Greenspan.

The dot-com failures, the stock market crash, and the start of the economic slowdown preceded the September 2001 terrorist events[3] (see Case 1.1). There was a sharp drop in stock prices, manufacturing production slowed, and—most important from a new economy perspective—orders for new high-tech equipment tanked. Unemployment began to rise, though productivity surprisingly continued to grow.

Arguably, the recession was a consequence of excesses related to the Internet and telecom boom of the late 1990s. The September 2001 terrorist attack brought many of the underlying problems into stark relief, and in 2002 the accounting machinations that some firms had used to turn losses into pro forma profits undermined investor confidence. That left even the most optimistic new economy supporters worried about a "double dip" recession, one dip following an earlier one, with no more than a token intervening recovery.

Nevertheless, the *Economist* provides a summary view based on a reader survey:

> *"Instead of running for 50 to 60 years at time, as they have done since the 18th century, long waves of industrial activity lately have been coming thicker and faster. The present one, which started in the late 1980s following the widespread introduction of computer networking and gathered momentum as the industrial world embraced the Internet, is expected to last for no more than 25 years, fizzling out in 2010 to 2015. So what was that crashing sound in April 2000, when America's technology-dominated NASDAQ stock market plummeted and wiped out countless dot-com and telecoms firms that imagined they could defy gravity? Jarring as it was, our readers believe it was just the crunch of gears that occurs when the heady upswing part of a Schumpeter cycle gives way to more mature growth. The present cycle—the fifth since the Industrial Revolution—has not even peaked."[4]*

---

[3]The National Bureau of Economic Research, which officially dates business cycle turns, set the start of the recession at March 2001. However, there were plenty of signs of a slowing economy before that date. Stock prices had already peaked in March 2000, industrial production began to decline in September 2000, etc.

[4]*Economist,* December 8, 2001. *<http://www.economics.com>*.

Recession and stock market crash notwithstanding, what are the defining characteristics of the new economy? Here are some:

- Rapid technological change, particularly in application of new e-technologies to a broad range of sectors.

- Increased competition, arising not only from new technologies but also from better communication and greater market scope.

- Improvement in the pace of productivity growth.

- Emphasis on employing white-collar brainpower rather than physical mass production.

- Reorganization of business to take advantages of economies of scale and scope.

- Exports of intellectual services—patent licenses, consulting, and financial intermediation—rather than exports of goods.

Behind the hypotheses about improved aggregate economic performance lie profound changes in business organization as a result of changes in information technology. The IT revolution has stretched over many years. It developments are closely dependent on one another, yet they affect very different sectors of the economy.

- In the beginning, progress in the basic sciences led to inventions like transistors, integrated circuits, digital electronics, fiberoptics, and software. Some of these advances occurred in university laboratories, but some critical ones took place in laboratories in large corporations, like Bell Labs (now part of Lucent) or IBM. Year after year the progress has been astonishingly rapid; think of the vastly increasing number of transistors that can be crowded on a single chip, the number of messages that can travel on a single strand of fiberoptic cable, the density of computer memory. And the progress in basic and applied science continues.

- Technical innovation was necessary to turn laboratory inventions into practical new products like PCs, laptops, routers, servers, memory devices, and cell phones. That called for types of expertise entirely different from basic science. Still other expertise is required to commercialize and mass-produce products beyond the development stage.

- The need for operating and applications software distinguishes the new technology from past technical achievements like railroads and electric motors, whose use relied on human judgment or skill. Today's computers, cell phones, and much electronic and mechanical equipment (even some automobiles!) rely on software to perform useful functions. Emerging computer languages like Fortran and Cobol represented substantial progress early on.[5] Originally, software was written for a unique use. Business applications were proprietary and operated only on a firm's own computer system. The monumental step was software that allowed different systems to speak to one another, creating a network of operating systems, communication programs, management programs, and myriads of other applications. From an economic and commercial perspective, these are altogether different products from hardware. Their development may call for investment in high-skill programming, but their proliferation is relatively costless.

Manufacturing, commercial distribution, and servicing are critical in building a community of users who are interconnected by a network. Fabrication of chips and assembly of computer hardware is rapidly moving from advanced countries like the United States and Japan, where the products were first developed, to production sites in lower-wage countries in Latin America and East Asia. Programming is still largely, though not entirely (as we will see), being carried on in Silicon Valley, Seattle, Austin, Boston, and other spots in the developed world.

The next stage is the e-business revolution. It lies in applying computer-based programs to business tasks that would otherwise have to be performed by human intervention. The potential for replacing clerks who operate calculating machines (abacuses in some countries) and writing orders and receipts on paper (sometimes with numerous carbons) is very large, perhaps far greater than the productivity gains in the IT industries themselves and affecting parts of the economy beyond the technical IT sectors.

The largest potential productivity gains are in conventional industries. This is the bulk of e-business potential. Some of the gains result from doing old tasks in new ways—stock brokerage transactions on the Internet, for example. Others are new types of businesses altogether. Some of the most important gains for consumers cannot be fully measured, among them the informational gains from the World Wide Web (WWW).

The evolution towards e-business has stretched over many years; its stages tend to interact in virtuous circles. New technology yields newer and more efficient hardware. In turn, that permits more sophisticated complex software. That in turn creates potential for new e-businesses. The profits from hardware and from applications provide incentives for new ventures.

---

[5]A "family tree" diagram and detailed discussions of the development of almost 50 computer languages are available at *<http://www.google.com/search?q=ache:ug D6UKCxEvOC:perso.wanadoo.fr/levenel/lang/+%22computer+22&hl=en&ie=UTF-8>*.

While much progress has been made, many of the possibilities have only barely been touched. New technical developments such as integration of audio and video communication and computers are still to come. E-business possibilities include automation of the supply chain from producer to consumer.

Finally, as IT and e-business mature, there is substantial continued work to be done in servicing and updating new hardware and software. This remains a challenge long after new systems have been installed and put to work.

We will be looking in greater detail below at forces driving the e-business revolution that affect the organization and operation of business, among them:

- Network interconnectivity.
- Instant communication.
- Knowledge bases.
- Externalities.
- Declining costs.
- Economies of scale.
- Reduced transaction costs.
- Competitive and anticompetitive forces.
- Globalization.

Business managers are aware of the opportunities *and* challenges resulting from the e-business revolution; like us, many of them continue to see bright possibilities.

Case 1.1
The 2001 Recession and the Dot-com Crash

After the stock market peaked in March 2000, its crash and the recession that followed brought to an end the longest and in recent years most buoyant boom. According to economic columnist Paul Krugman, "The recession of 2001 wasn't a typical postwar slump brought on when an inflation-fighting Fed raises interest rates . . . his was a prewar-style recession brought on by irrational exuberance."[6] Most postwar recessions followed the Federal Reserve's efforts to bring down inflation by raising interest rates. The result was a temporary drop in investment and an inventory cycle. Once inflationary pressures had subsided and the Fed reduced rates, residential construction and con-

---

[6]Paul Krugman. "Dubya's Double Dip?" *New York Times,* August 2, 2002.

sumer spending would snap back and before long—though sometimes it seemed a long, long time—business investment recovered.

This time around, it was different. Inflationary pressures showed little sign of building (perhaps a mark of the new economy), and the Fed did not tighten money (see Case 2.1). The recession resulted from the collapse of an over-heated boom, some of it in high-tech products like fiberoptic cable and routers and some of it in the "soft" parts of e-business. The implication is that a solid recovery awaits strong business investment, but Krugman feels that "Most businesses are in no hurry to go on another spending spree."

Signs of a slowdown—fewer new orders for and less investment in com-puters, unanticipated inventory accumulation—preceded the turn toward neg-ative GDP growth during the first three quarters of 2001 (Figure 1.1). Even at its lowest point, GDP was only 0.6 percent lower than at its peak. This has been a relatively short and modest decline—though another dip of recession, which is widely feared, could make the slowdown more serious.

Figure 1.1: The 2001 Recession: Percent Change in Real GDP

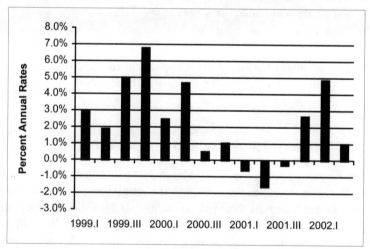

An inventory swing, typical of most recessions, accounts for much of the recessionary pattern of GDP. This time, the reduction in inventories was abrupt and the inventory adjustment lasted only a short time, a more volatile pattern than in past recessions.[7] Perhaps this reflects the fact that electronic inventory

---

[7]J. A. Kahn and M. M. McConnell, "Has Inventory Volatility Returned? A Look at the Current Cycle." *Current Issues in Economics and Finance* (8) 5: 1-6, Federal Reserve Bank of New York.

control has made it possible for firms to get along with smaller inventories and has enabled them to spot and respond to excessive inventory buildups more quickly. Consumer spending and residential construction stayed strong—a surprise considering the adverse impacts on expectations in connection with the terrorism attacks and the corporate accounting fraud problems that began to appear late in 2001.

A drastic decline in the stock market affected high-tech, telecom, and Internet stocks much more severely than stocks of old economy firms (see Figure 1.2). The IT fields that had been most directly involved in the boom of the 1990s have been the hardest hit since. There was clearly a bubble whose bursting reduced many stock values to a small fraction of their peak values, even in a number of cases to zero.

Figure 1.2: The Dot-Com Crash

Chart 2-8 Equity Prices
Led by the technology-heavy NASDAQ, stock markets continued to record large gains in 1999. Internet stocks skyrocketed.

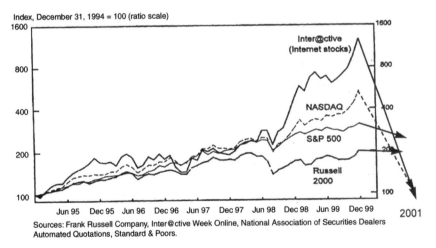

Sources: Frank Russell Company, Inter@ctive Week Online, National Association of Securities Dealers Automated Quotations, Standard & Poors.

It is not possible to measure the collapse of the dot-com firms—many of which were not yet publicly owned corporations—as they failed to make their revenue projections and found their venture capital being withdrawn. Hearsay evidence suggests that a very large number of new ventures were affected. Many enterprises in Silicon Valley have closed and their workers have been scattered. While the loss in terms of operating organizations and accumulated knowledge is incalculable, many entrepreneurs are undoubtedly standing in the wings plotting their next moves.

Prospects for the future were clouded by slow recovery of demand for electronic equipment, telecoms, and programming services. This is not surprising given the overwhelming surplus capacity built up in the boom years. Fears of a double dip recession or of only a slow recovery were themselves a barrier to a return to rapid growth because investors have been reluctant to acquire more hardware or to make long-term commitments to new programming systems. Forecasting even the short-term future has been difficult. On the one hand, immediate prospects for a quick recovery of investment and e-business spending look clouded. On the other hand, many opportunities have not yet been exploited and rapid changes in technology will create new investment opportunities.

Chapter 2
Is There Statistical Evidence for a New Economy?

There is still much disagreement among economists about the results and the importance of the changes that are occurring. Many experts note that in recent years productivity has increased more rapidly than it previously did, but others have taken the position that this does not signal a new era because more rapid productivity growth may reflect poor measurement or may be a consequence of the fast cyclical expansion of the economy in the late 1990s. What does the evidence show?

We focus first on the growth of output and productivity, because more rapid economic progress is widely seen as the defining event of the new economy. Then we turn to the trade-off between inflation and unemployment—the question of whether the new era makes it possible for unemployment to drop to new lows without provoking inflation. Finally, we look at the business cycle: Is there a basis for saying that the business cycle has been attenuated? Could it even be entirely gone?

A TREND TOWARD HIGHER PRODUCTIVITY?

In recent years, perceptions of the U.S. economy have changed dramatically. In the 1970s and 1980s, most observers would have described the United States as having a mature economy, one that was having difficulties adapting to new economic realities. Mass production manufacturing, especially our famed auto industry, was doing badly, struggling unsuccessfully to meet foreign competition. Productivity growth had slowed precipitously from its rapid expansion of the first two postwar decades to just 1.4 percent a year. The 1970s in particular were a time of energy shortages; there were oil shocks in 1974 and in 1979-80, when sharp increases in energy prices caused inflation, unemployment, and recession.

The 1990s, in contrast, were characterized by a new dynamism. Even as Europe was still in the grip of "eurosclerosis" and Japan suffered from repeated recessions, growth in the United States was no longer sluggish. In the five years from 1995 to 2000, productivity grew at 2.9 percent per year—twice the average productivity growth for the years from 1973 through 1995. The mature economy had gained a second wind!

Figures 2.1 and 2.2 show output and productivity changes in the U.S. economy after 1970. Figure 2.1 shows the movement of real GDP (the solid line), and the potential output trends (the straight dashed lines). Average annual growth from 1973 to 1995 is 1.4 percent. The steeper trend line fitted to data from 1995 to 1999 follows the much faster growth path of 2.9 percent a year. But does this really represent a structural break in traditional patterns that will be maintained in spite of the dot-com crash? The solid line shows the ups and downs of the business cycle. Note that the recent more rapid growth trend corresponds to a period of expansion in the business cycle.

Figure 2.1: Potential and Actual Output Trends

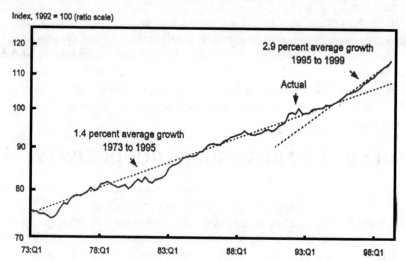

Index, 1992 = 100 (ratio scale)

Note: Productivity is the average of income- and product-side measures. Productivity for 1999 is inferred from the first three quarters.
Sources: Department of Commerce (Bureau of Economic Analysis) and Department of Labor (Bureau of Labor Statistics).

Source: Economic Report of the President, 2001.

Figure 2.2 looks at the same developments from a somewhat different angle. The statistics represent the percentage change in output per worker over many years. Productivity growth is very cyclical; the low points correspond to recessions and the high points match periods of rapid growth. That is easy to explain: Characteristically, in a boom new workers are not hired as quickly as production increases, so there is a gain in output per worker. During downswings, layoffs lag behind declines in output; each worker is producing less, so output per worker falls off in a recession.

Figure 2.2: U.S. Business Productivity Growth, 1977-2001

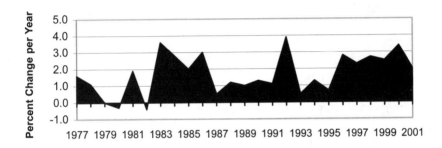

Source: Economic Report of the President 2001 and Economic Indicators, July 2002.

It is not altogether surprising that some people are skeptical about a new upward trend in productivity. The improvement in productivity since 1996 corresponds mostly to a business upswing. The 2002 revisions of the national accounts show business nonfarm output per man-hour growing at between 2.5 and 3.5 percent from 1996 through 2000. As the saying goes, "One swallow does not make a summer." Nor does one business and productivity upswing make a long-term trend. However, productivity growth continued in 2001 and 2002 even when it might have been expected it to decline as the economy fell into recession (Table 2.1). At best, the aggregate productivity data are only a very tentative "yes" vote for those who support the hypothesis that there is a new economy.

On the other side, a leading opponent of the new economy idea, Robert Gordon of Northwestern University, argues that recent higher productivity growth figures largely reflect productivity improvements that could naturally be expected to result from the economy's rapid growth in the late 1990s. Moreover, Gordon notes that while improvements in semiconductor technology clearly led to rapid productivity improvement in electronic hardware (computers and communications equipment), they are hard to discern elsewhere in

Table 2.1: Quarterly Productivity Growth, 1999-2002
(nonfarm business output per man-hour)
(quarterly changes at annual percentage rates)

	% Annual Rate
1999: I	2.4
II	-0.8
III	3.7
IV	6.3
2000: I	0.2
II	6.0
III	0.6
IV	1.7
2001: I	-1.5
II	-0.1
III	2.1
IV	7.3
2002:I	8.6
II	1.7
III *	5.5
IV e	-0.2

Source: Economic Indicators, November 2002.
*Provisional

the economy.[1] In fact, while the capabilities of high-tech products like chips have been increasing prodigiously, very little productivity gain has so far been measured in older sectors of the economy.

Various studies have tried to disentangle the productivity acceleration of the 1995-2000 period by applying statistical theory. The estimates, summarized in Table 2.2, take broadly similar approaches: The idea is to explain the improvement in productivity, output per hour, in terms of the contributions of capital and of labor quality. No explicit allowance is made for measurement problems or cyclical factors.

The unexplained remainder, usually called total factor productivity (TFP), represents productivity gains that cannot be explained in terms of production inputs like labor and capital. TFP is usually associated with technological change, though it may also represent the effect of other forces, such as an

[1]Robert J. Gordon (2000). "Does the New Economy Measure up to the Great Inventions of the Past?" *Journal of Economic Perspectives,* 4 (14): 40-74.

increase in the scale of production or improved management. Many of the gains from the new economy might be expected to show up in this category.

Table 2.2: Disentangling the 1995-2000 Productivity Increase (percent per year)

	1973-1995	Acceleration of Labor Productivity Growth (% per year in 1995-2000 less % per year, 1973-1995)		
		Oliner/ Sichel	*Baily/ Lawrence*	*Jorgenson/ Ho/Stiroh*
Labor productivity contribution of:	1.4	1.08	1.26	0.92
Total capital	0.7	0.34	0.44	0.52
IT capital	0.4	0.59	0.59	0.44
Other capital	0.3	-0.25	-0.15	0.08
Labor quality	0.2	0.04	0.04	-0.11
Total factor productivity (TFP)	0.4	0.72	0.82	0.51
Computer sector TFP		0.47	0.18	0.27
Other sector TFP		0.25	0.64	0.24

Note: Contributions do not add up exactly because growth rates are combined by multiplication.

Sources: Adapted from M. N. Baily (2002). "The New Economy: Post Mortem or Second Wind?" paper presented at the meetings of the American Economic Association, Atlanta, GA, January 4-6, 2002; Stephen D. Oliner and Daniel E. Sichel (2000). "The Resurgence of Growth in the Late 1990s: Is Information Technology the Story?" *Journal of Economic Perspectives* 14 (4): 3-32; M. N. Baily and Robert Lawrence (2001). "Do We Have a New Economy?" *American Economic Review: Papers and Proceedings,* 91 (2): 308-12; Dale W. Jorgenson, Ho Mun, and Kevin J. Stiroh, (2001). "Projecting Productivity Growth: Lessons from the U.S. Growth Resurgence," paper for the conference on "Technology, Growth, and the Labor Market," Federal Reserve Bank of Atlanta, January 7, 2002.

Table 2.2 shows first the average growth figures for the 1973-95 period, generally acknowledged to have been a time of slow productivity growth, which is sometimes used as a marker of a mature economy. Then we show the improvement as measured in various studies analyzing the difference between the economy's performance in the 1995-2000 period and the 1973-1995 period. All the studies show a gain in labor productivity of more or less 1 percent. In other words, during 1995-2000, average annual output per man-hour increased by 2 to 2.5 percent compared to an annual average of 1.4 percent in the previous two decades.

How much of this gain can be attributed to "capital deepening"—investment in more capital-intensive and complex machinery? The studies found the effect of greater capital intensity to be more or less 0.5 percent, with most of that effect attributable to IT investments, including those in software; this was the result of the investment boom in computers, fiberoptic cables, and sophisticated software systems. On the next line, changes in labor quality have only little more impact recently than in the past because improvements in the educational attainment of workers have been proceeding apace for many years.

The remainder represents TFP, the gains in productivity that are not explained by capital deepening or change in labor quality. TFP accounted for only 0.4 percent of annual total productivity growth of 1.4 percent in the 1973-1995 period. It appears to be considerably higher, almost 0.75 percent, in 1995-2000. This represents the productivity gain attributable to the new economy.[2]

Experts differ about how much of the gain originates in the computer sector and how much comes from spillovers to the rest of the economy. In the words of the IMF: "The main outstanding issue is whether IT has contributed to TFP growth more generally by increasing the efficiency of production, either through usage or knowledge spillovers.... The debate focuses on whether the remainder of the acceleration [of labor productivity} reflects cyclical factors or an increase in underlying TFP growth."[3] How much e-business is contributing to productivity growth depends on the answer to this question.

Other studies of the performance of specific sectors are suggestive but not conclusive. Outside the IT-producing industries, sectors like banking, retail trade, and wholesale trade that made the heaviest investments in IT in the early 1990s later showed the largest gains in labor productivity. It may take time for the effects of IT investments to affect productivity.[4]

Are there corresponding statistical results for other countries? Considering how rapidly computer and communications technology has spread across the world, comparable improvements should be expected elsewhere. IMF studies of individual countries[5] show some acceleration of productivity growth in Australia but not in other major economies like Japan, France, the United

---

[2]A similar calculation in the 2002 *Economic Report* shows a much higher TFP gain, most of which is attributed to sectors other than computers, but the result is improbable because it relies heavily on the unlikely assumption that structural productivity growth in the 1995-2001 period has been understated by approximately 0.5 percent as a result of cyclical factors. Because TFP and TFP attributable to noncomputer sectors are calculated by subtraction, all of this assumed value appears in the bottom line, as an increase in productivity in the noncomputer sectors of almost 1.5 percent a year.

[3]International Monetary Fund, *World Economic Outlook: The Information Technology Revolution.* Washington, DC: Oct. 2001, p. 112; <*http://www.imf.org/external/pubs/ft/weo/2001/02/pdf/chapter3.pdf*>.

[4]Ibid.

[5]Ibid.

Kingdom, and the East Asian countries. Nevertheless, in some of these cases business cycle weakness may be offsetting the effects of the IT revolution.

More recently, reviewing its 26 member countries, the OECD also found that recent growth has been quite uneven, a pattern that can be related only in part to IT.[6] Some countries showed spectacular improvements in the 1990s, particularly the second half; among them are the United States, Ireland, the Netherlands, and Australia. Others, like Japan and Germany, have shown slower growth even after allowance is made for business cycle movements.

A number of factors may account for these differences. Specifically, the improved growth in some countries reflects the application of new advanced technology products in various lines of business. In others, gains in productivity appear to result from accumulation of more capital and an improvement in the quality of the work force. The OECD is particularly concerned about structural rigidities in the business and labor markets in some European countries.

We can thus conclude that in the United States, but not everywhere in the world, there is evidence of an improvement in TFP attributable to new economy considerations. We cannot be sure how much of this occurs in the IT industries and how much is a spillover to the rest of the economy. Of necessity, statistical analysis so far focuses on the relatively short recent period since 1996. Since it takes a long time for new techniques to be introduced, not enough time has passed to make the answer clear. Statistical studies are producing promising evidence but they do not yet provide unqualified support for the thesis that IT-related technological change is responsible for a persistent trend of higher productivity.

Case Study 2.1
The Productivity Paradox

"You can see the computer age everywhere but in the productivity statistics," Robert Solow said some time ago.[7] This widely quoted statement is commonly referred to as the Solow Productivity Paradox. When it was made in 1987, economists were trying to explain an apparent slowdown in United States productivity growth in the 1970s and 1980s: From 1948 to 1973 labor productivity had grown at an annual rate of 2.9 percent, but from 1974 to the end of the 1980s, it grew only 1.1 percent per year. Solow saw that the productivity statistics did not reflect the rapid introduction of computers. More recent-

---

[6]Organization for Economic Cooperation and Development (2001). *The New Economy: Beyond the Hype.* Paris: OECD.
[7]Robert Solow. "We'd Better Watch Out." *New York Times Book Review*, July 12, 1987, p. 36.

ly, since 1996, productivity growth has accelerated to 2.6 percent a year. Today, Solow might have a different opinion, though I do not know whether he would agree that there is a new economy.

Was there really a paradox? How can it be explained?

Though the productivity statistics supported Solow's hypothesis, there is no universal agreement among economists that there was indeed a paradox.[8] The slowdown in productivity growth during the 1970s and 1980s may well reflect the economic/political difficulties of the period, the oil crisis, and the inflationary pressures that resulted. Productivity growth could have declined even if the introduction of computer had had positive effects.

Moreover, though in 1987 computers were widespread, they made up only a relatively small fraction of total capital. It has been argued that the use of hedonic price indexes (explained below) to allow for changes in computer quality would overstate the quantity of computers. Yet as we discuss elsewhere in this chapter, the price index for computers declined very rapidly. If the estimates of the decline in computer prices were too big, statistics on the output of computers would be overstated. They might not really have been "everywhere."

Even if computers did seem to be everywhere, it can be argued that it took time for computers to influence productivity. They had to be perfected, they had to be diffused throughout the market, and how to use them had to be learned. As in other fundamental economic revolutions, the impact of the computer could well have been delayed; as one commentator responded: "You don't see computers in the productivity statistics yet, but wait a bit and you will."[9]

Other possibilities are that the advantages of computers do not show up in the economic statistics or that they are not as productive "as you think." This refers to the fact that the gains in personal productivity—through finding information on the Web, for example— associated with computers may be large but, as we know, when all is said and done, computers are still imperfect; they demand much learning and they have many glitches.

So where do we come out today on the productivity paradox?

In the days just before the dot-com crash, people were talking about "the productivity growth spurt in the United States."[10] As we

[8]For a discussion see Jack E. Tripplet, "The Solow Productivity Paradox: What do Computers do to Productivity?" *Canadian Journal of Economics* 32 (2): 309-34.
[9]Tripplet, op. cit., p.2.
[10]This was in fact the title of remarks by Federal Reserve Governor Edward M. Gramlich on February 2, 2001.

have noted, productivity growth is affected by the business cycle. In a recession we would expect slower, even negative, productivity growth. While productivity growth has been maintained in recent quarters, it is too soon to be sure of a return to the rapid growth rates of the late 1990s. The important thing is that the proliferation of net-worked computer communication and e-business is still underway. The dynamic of the economy continues, though temporarily at a slow-er pace. It will be interesting to see if, in the coming decade, we will see a return to productivity paradox views.

PRICE, COST, AND OUTPUT MEASUREMENT IN THE NEW ECONOMY

Moore's law (Case 3.1) suggests that each successive generation of semicon-ductors is much more powerful than the previous ones. That usually means that they have greater capacity—that they are faster and better. Yet, after an initial introductory period, the new chips are typically no more expensive than the old. In effect, then, the real price of chips has been falling rapidly:

"The economics of semiconductors begins with the closely related observation that semiconductors have become cheaper at a truly staggering rate! Between 1974 and 1996 prices of memory chips decreased by a factor of 7,270 times, or at 40.9 percent per year, while the implicit deflator for the gross domestic product (GDP) increased by 1.3 times or 4.6 percent per year! Semiconductor price declines closely parallel Moore's Law on the growth of chip capacity"[11]

The sharp decline in the prices of computers and memory and logic chips is shown in Figure 2.3.

The challenge for the new economy of measuring prices and real outputs is that products are changing. It would not make sense simply to compare the price of this year's computer with the price of a computer produced last year, because the product has undergone substantial improvement. So how much of the price change represents change in product specifications and how much represents a true change in price?

---

[11]Dale W. Jorgenson (2001). "Information Technology and the U.S. Economy." *American Economic Review*, 94 (1): 1-32, at 3.

Figure 2.3: Relative Prices of Computers and Semiconductors, 1959-1999

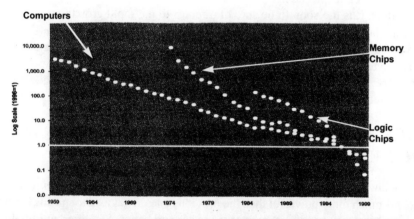

Source: D. Jorgenson (2001). "Information Technology and the U. S. Economy." *American Economic Review,* 94 (1): 1-32. (All prices relative to output price.)

The Bureau of Labor Statistics (BLS) and the Bureau of Economic Analysis (BEA), with the help of economists from IBM, have devised matched model and hedonic index techniques to allow for product change. Matched model methods use products with comparable specifications in two years (the matched models) to establish a measure of the price change that occurred over the two-year period. Hedonic indexes relate prices to the underlying characteristics of the products—in the case of computers, largely memory capacity and speed. This makes it possible to hold the qualities of products constant from one year to the next so that price change can be measured.

Analyzing the extremely rapid changes taking place in specifications of electronic products while nominal prices remain roughly fixed, the computed quality-adjusted price indexes suggest extremely rapid price decline. These kinds of price measures have recently been introduced into U.S. price indexes and into the national accounts statistics for computers and peripheral equipment, semiconductors, communications equipment, and prepackaged software (but not for own-account or custom software).

The rapid measured declines in the prices of electronic equipment and software have important consequences in measuring real output and productivity. The basic measurement of national accounts begins by using a price index to deflate current price data and proceeds to obtain real output data. Even if production is flat measured by nominal value, a declining price measure would suggest that real output has been increasing. This is pretty much the case with IT equipment.

In other words, the increase in output and productivity may reflect the way we measure. On this basis, as we have mentioned, some economists like Gordon disallow a large share of recent productivity improvement as being simply the result of the measurement technique used. Gordon argues that he cannot type any faster with his fancy new computer!

Growth rates of prices and quantities for GDP and various components of investment and consumption, as estimated by Dale Jorgenson of Harvard, are shown in Table 2.3.

Table 2.3: Growth Rates of Output and Prices

| | Percent Changes per Year | | | |
| | 1990-1995 | | 1995-1999 | |
	Prices	**Quantities**	**Prices**	**Quantities**
Gross domestic product	1.99	2.36	1.62	4.08
Information technology	-4.42	12.15	-9.74	20.75
Computers	-15.77	21.71	-12.09	38.81
Software	-1.62	11.86	-2.43	20.8
Communications equipment	-1.77	7.01	-2.9	11.42
Information technology services	-2.95	12.19	-11.76	18.24
Noninformation technology investment	2.15	1.22	2.2	4.21
Noninformation technology consumption	2.35	2.06	2.3	2.79

Source: D. Jorgenson, 2001. "Information Technology and the U. S. Economy." *American Economic Review,* 94 (1): 1-32.

In the second half of the 1990s, average annual GDP grew somewhat more rapidly than in the first half, a little over 4 percent compared to 2.4 percent; price increases ran between 1.5 and 2.0 percent in both periods. The very different performance of IT products, particularly computers, is striking. These showed massive reductions in price and increases in quantity—real computer output increased at an annual rate of 38.8 percent and prices were reduced at an annual rate of 12.1 percent in the 1995-99 period. Other IT products show somewhat smaller price declines and correspondingly smaller increases in quantity.

The question is whether the adjustment for price change is the principal source of the measured increase in output. That is not likely. Computer and peripheral equipment output has increased even if we simply count the number of boxes produced without adjustment for quality change. Lower effective prices have stimulated purchasing. The improved quality of computers and other IT products must be taken into account in measuring the nation's product.

On the other hand, adjustments for quality change significantly affect the real output figures. If they are too large, prices would be too low and output too high. Is the new economy simply a figment of the statisticians' imagination? We think not, but it is important to be cautious about evaluating the statistics.[12]

Similar quality questions arise with respect to sectors outside the IT field. Improved technology and software have brought monumental improvements in communication, in financial transactions, and in retail ordering. Cell phones, computerized bank accounts, and B2C transactions illustrate the point. These add greatly to the convenience of life—we are indeed better off—but many of these improvements are not measured in GDP.[13] This suggests that important aspects of the new economy remain unmeasured. If they were to be measured, the growth and productivity figures would be larger.

Another perspective on measurement is that of Brynjolfsson and Hitt.[14] Looking at firm-level data, they argue that the aggregate statistics greatly understate the actual gain in productivity. Their views are consistent with Gordon's views on price measurement: The prices of new, scientifically complex, products like computers are difficult to measure. At best, the adjustments we make for improved performance and quality can only be arbitrary.

Brynjolfsson and Hitt are concerned with the complementarity between hardware costs and the organizational costs of computerization. Very large investments in intangible assets are necessary to make the new computerized systems work.[15] They includes investment not only in programming but also in reorganizing and rebuilding business processes and in training personnel.

---

[12]In most European countries, national accounts statisticians do not yet adjust prices of IT products for quality change; European national accounts statistics also do not do not show the late 1990s improved productivity trend that we observe in the United States.

[13]This applies to gains going to final users. To the extent that these gains affect the costs of production, they should reduce prices and show up in real output.

[14]Erik Brynjolfsson & Lorin M. Hitt (2000). "Beyond Computation: Information Technology, Organizational Transformation, and Business Performance." *Journal of Economic Perspectives,* 14 (4): 23-48; <*http://ebusiness.mit.edu/erik*>.

[15]On the basis of firm-level studies, the ratio of intangible to tangible assets invested in computerization may as large at 10 to 1. Erik Brynjolfsson & S. Yang (1997). "The Intangible Costs and Benefits of Computer Investments: Evidence from Financial Markets." Proceedings of the International Conference on Information Systems. Software is now being capitalized in computing the national accounts, but other intangible expenses are not.

Substantial costs are incurred in hiring consultants and in compensating employees for additional time.

Such upfront costs, which are usually measured as current expense, are counted against current output at the firm level. Most of these expenditures for improving business processes and improving worker skills will pay off over time, often over periods as long as seven years. These intangible investments should be counted as part of output and later depreciated. "To the extent that this net capital accumulation has not been counted as part of output, output and output growth have been underestimated."[16] Brynjolfsson and Hitt estimate that during periods of rapid change, this underestimate of the GDP growth rate could exceed 1.0 percent a year.

The information on productivity change is suggestive. It is unlikely that all the improvement in productivity reflects price adjustment—and if it did, it would be the result of quality improvements. Moreover, there is reason to think that some productivity improvements associated with IT and e-business slip through without being measured.

FULL EMPLOYMENT WITHOUT INFLATION

An improved trade-off between inflation and unemployment is thought to be another empirical dimension of the new economy. One of the challenges of macroeconomic policymaking is to push the economy as close to full employment as possible without provoking inflation. On the basis of the experience of the 1970s and 1980s, U.S. economic policy makers had focused on 6 percent unemployment as a reasonable target: they believed that once unemployment was reduced below 6 percent, sometimes termed the NAIRU (nonaccelerating inflation rate of unemployment), inflationary pressures would begin to mount.

The trade-off between inflation and the unemployment rate is called the Phillips curve (see Figure 2.4). The closer an economy is to full employment (the lower the unemployment rate), the higher the rate of inflation. This is a notably fragile relationship.

Originally thought to be stable by its inventor, A. W. Phillips, the curve has turned out to be quite variable. The Phillips curve has been known to shift as a result of changes in input prices or expectations. The curve farthest to the right (II), for example, might represent the 1970s period of the oil crisis when inflationary pressures and expectations were high. The 1990s are shown by curves I and III: The arrows point to a shift of the curve downward to the left, from curve I in the early 1990s to curve III in the late 1990s. This would mean

---

[16]Brynjolfsen & Hitt, op. cit.

a move favorable inflation/unemployment trade-off, like the one we have seen
in recent years (see Figure 2.5). The question is:

    Was this a significant lasting shift and can it be attributed to the new econ-
omy?

Figure 2.4: The Relationship between Inflation and Unemployment: The Phillips Curve

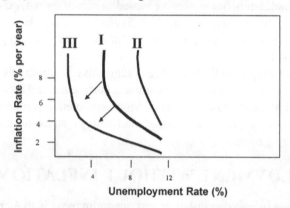

Figure 2.5: Tradeoff between Inflation and Unemployment

    The data on unemployment and inflation do suggest that the Phillips curve
constraint seems to have been lifted in the late 1990s. This is apparent in
Figure 2.5, which shows the inflation rate (the rate of growth of the Consumer
Price Index [CPI]) on the vertical axis and the unemployment rate on the hor-
izontal.

Each point stands for the inflation and unemployment data for one year, from 1970 to 2001. The points that correspond to 1997-2001 are in the circle on the lower left. The points that correspond to the oil crisis years in the 1970s and early 1980s are in the circle in the upper right. The points around the middle of the chart, not circled, are the data for the late 1980s and early 1990s, a "normal" period.

The late 1990s, as seen in the circle on the left, clearly represent a more favorable time; the rates of both inflation *and* unemployment were lower than earlier. Technological progress was producing increased gains in productivity that offset increased wages. In other words, as a result of improved productivity, businesses could pay higher hourly wages without passing them on to their customers as higher prices. Using this new economy reasoning as a justification, the Federal Reserve allowed the economy to expand to allow for lower rates of unemployment than had earlier been thought possible—less than 4 percent—without applying monetary policy "brakes" (see Case 2.2).

Is a new economy a good explanation for what happened in the late 1990s? Again, our answer must be "yes and no."

Yes, there clearly has been a shift in the Phillips curve. It reflects not only the sharp decline in computer and IT prices but also an easing of general price pressures. Gains in productivity, in part the result of IT technology, allowed businesses to make higher profits and pay higher wages without raising prices. This is clearly a new economy phenomenon.

The changing composition of production away from manufacturing toward knowledge-based products has also modified requirements for capital and for labor. White-collar workers, who play a larger role in high-tech fields, have specialized skills. Their salaries and employment are less likely to be sensitive to general labor market conditions than the wages of production line workers. That may also help to explain why wages and prices have not been as quick to rise in response to full employment as in the past.

But no, the shift of the Phillips curve may have little to do with the new economy. After a long period of relative price stability, price and inflationary expectations have fallen. Moreover, the labor force has aged. Because older workers change jobs less often than young workers, they have fewer periods of temporary unemployment. It may be, therefore, that in today's labor market an unemployment rate of about 4 percent is the equivalent of an unemployment rate of 6 percent early in the 1990s. That would also explain the shift in the Phillips curve.

On balance, however, it seems that new economy factors have had a significant impact and that the shift in the Phillips curve may be related to the new economy. The difficulty is that we cannot be sure that a more favorable Phillips curve will persist; in a continued recession, cost pressures may cause the curve to shift up once again.

IS THE BUSINESS CYCLE DEAD?

Though the recession of 2001 is evidence that the business cycle is still very much with us, business cycle patterns may have been changed by the new economy. Figure 2.6 shows various indicators of business cycle conditions. The dark bars in the chart represent periods of recession. The recessions of the 1970s and early 1980s are very apparent. After the 1990-91 recession, there was a long period of uninterrupted expansion, from 1991 to 2001.

Figure 2.6: Indicators of U.S. Business Cycles

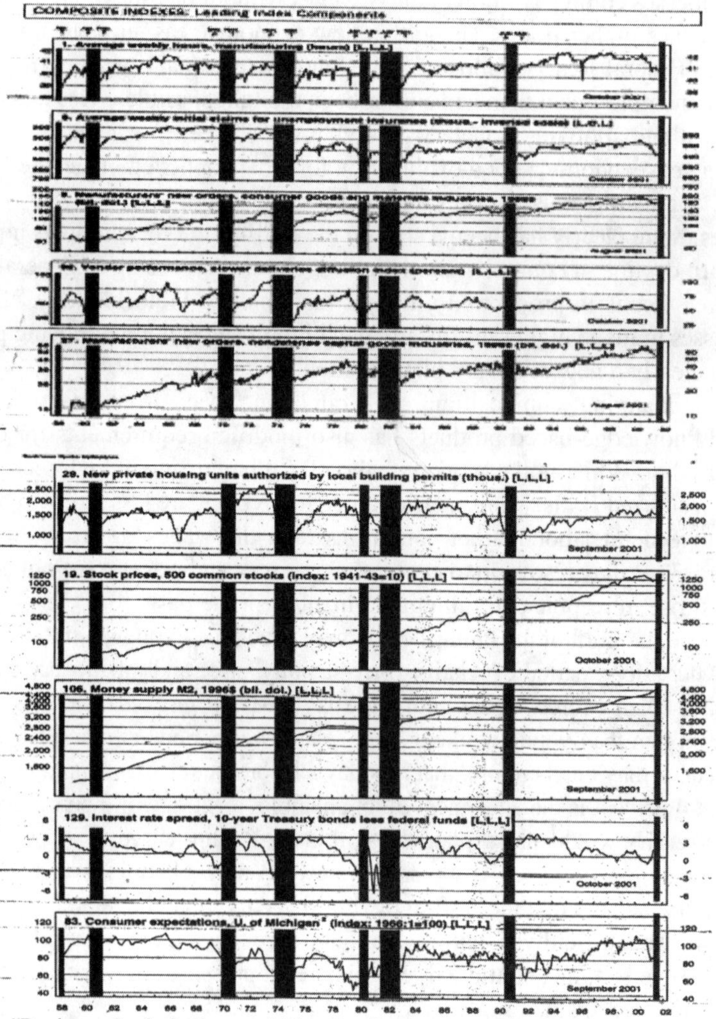

Source: "Business Cycle Indicators." The Conference Board, June 2002.

The cyclical volatility of these indicators varies greatly; some—like average weekly hours worked, new orders, and consumer expectations—mirror the business cycle closely. Others—like money supply—show a steady upward movement with little cyclical fluctuation.

The timing of the turning point toward recession of each series varies depending on which variables are considered. The indicators shown here are all leading indicators selected on the basis that their movements often foreshadow a recession or a recovery. Note, for example, that average weekly hours, new orders, and stock prices declined well before the start of the 2001 recession. Indicators like consumer and investor expectations also signaled a downturn of the economy.

Averaging information on employment, orders, manufacturing activity, nonfarm output, and other contemporaneous measures of economic activity, the National Bureau of Economic Research, which makes these judgments, decided that the U.S. economy entered into recession in March 2001. (By February 2003the Bureau had not yet decided when the recession ended.) So much for the dream that the new economy would eliminate booms and busts.

The concept underlying the "business cycle is dead" theory was that in the new era businesses would be better able to match production and inventories to the current needs of the market. If financial experts could predict the future stream of profits, they might make accurate evaluations of stock prices, avoiding speculative bubbles and crashes. If business managers knew accurately how much product they would sell, they could schedule their supply chain management to make few mistakes. In a 1999 speech, Alan Greenspan said, "The dramatic changes in information technology that have enabled businesses to embrace the techniques of just-in-time inventory management appear to have reduced that part of the business cycle that is attributable to inventory fluctuations."[17] The idea is that thanks to IT, computer ordering, inventory control, and communication we would avoid the mismatch between production and demand and the accumulation of excessive inventories of the traditional business cycle. At least so we thought!

The massive liquidations of inventories that came quickly in the 2001 cycle[18] may be evidence of better inventory management, but other dimensions of the economy did not point toward improved rationality and control. The 2001 experience may indeed point in the opposite direction. It may reflect the fact that stock markets and investments in new IT-related activities remain more intuitive and less subject to management by computer information systems than inventories of traditional goods.

---

[17]Alan Greenspan (1999). "New Challenges for Monetary Policy." *<http://www.federal reserve.gov/boarddocs/speeches/speeches/1999/19990827.htm>*.
[18]Kahn and McConnell, op. cit, no. 7.

This business cycle has been different from previous cycles, reflecting the up and down of demand for high-tech capital goods. Note the long upswing of manufacturers' new orders, particularly for nondefense capital goods, and the decline in 2000, in advance of the official business cycle turning point.

"Irrational exuberance" and the greater ease and accessibility of doing stock market transactions on the Internet aggravated the stock market bubble in the late 1990s. Unrealistic expectations about the future potentials of untried e-businesses and the concomitant hope for enormous future profits may have caused business managers to venture further and to invest more than was wise. Even production schedules often seem to have been determined by unrealistic sales targets rather than by rational evaluations of what the market required. Practices like these may well amplify the likelihood and severity of business cycles. They seem to lie behind the stock market bubble and crash and the violent swing of investment spending that caused the 2001 recession. Numerous examples of the irrational expectations phenomenon lie behind the dot-com crash, which we discuss in more detail in Chapter 10.

It would obviously not be realistic to assume that the business cycle has disappeared. It is very much with us. On the other hand, the 1990s boom may well have lasted so long because of the IT revolution; an extended period of growth is consistent with a technological boom like the one in the late 1990s. Some optimists have argued that new information technology will result in faster inventory adjustments, leading to a shorter business cycle, one in which a recession may be more abrupt but the recovery will come more quickly. This is a view expressed by Fed Chairman Greenspan in his testimony to Congress in July 2002 when he said, "The mildness and brevity of the downturn are a testament to the notable improvement in the resilience and flexibility of the U.S. economy." But all the returns on the crash and recession are not yet in. . . .

Case 2.2
The Federal Reserve and the New Economy

"Five years ago, Alan Greenspan began pushing a reluctant Federal Reserve to embrace his new economy vision. . . . Today, Fed policymakers are debating whether they went too far. The answer could help determine whether the current recession is a temporary aberration in an era of swift growth, or whether the rapid growth of the late 1990s was itself the aberration. Mr. Greenspan hasn't lost the faith: "New capital investment, especially the high-tech type, will continue where it left off . . . the long-term outlook for productivity growth, as far as I'm concerned, remains substantially undiminished."[19]

---

[19]"Great Expectations: Did Greenspan Push High-Tech Optimism on Growth Too Far?" *Wall Street Journal,* December 28, 2001.

After the 1990s IT stock market boom collapsed, the economy declined into recession with growing unemployment, the September 11 terrorist attack, and many other negatives, serious experts even at the Fed began to question the new economy thesis. How did the Federal Reserve reach the consensus on the new economy that was the basis of its monetary policy until the end of 2000?

In 1995, Greenspan noted a surge in capital goods orders. His feeling that this would yield productivity gains that would permit faster growth without inflation was the basis for the Fed policy of low interest rates. This policy had the support of Alan Blinder, a more left-of-center economist appointed by President Clinton as Fed Vice Chairman in 1996, though Blinder did not sign on to the new economy thesis.

Others at the Fed expressed more skepticism. Board member Laurence Meyer argued in January 1998 that the previous year's growth was unsustainable. The Board's own research staff argued that the economy could not possibly grow at more than 2.5 percent a year without causing inflation. They explained rapid growth rates as a function of temporary factors that could not possibly persist. Outside experts, like Paul Romer of Stanford, also saw continued rapid growth as unrealistic.

But as rapid growth persisted without inflation in 1997, 1998, and 1999, the critics found Greenspan's new economy ideas hard to resist. Moreover, Greenspan sought support for his ideas by pushing efforts to update economic data, recognizing the problems of measuring productivity in such fields as banking and the high-tech industry. He thought that many companies were only at the beginning of a technological revolution and found many anecdotes supporting the opinion that the economy had changed fundamentally.

Many of Greenspan's once-skeptical colleagues came around to the view that capital spending would continue uninterrupted and that productivity growth would offset inflationary pressures.

Indeed, they may have been so persuaded by their rosy view of the future that they had trouble seeing early signs of a slowdown. Late in 2000, long after the stock market declined and excess capacity had built up in the telecom industry, the Fed staff was still projecting increases in outlays for equipment and software.

When the slowdown was finally recognized, in January 2001, the Fed quickly initiated interest rate cuts intended to keep the expansion from stalling. But the recession turned out more serious than expected, particularly in new economy high-tech fields. (The excesses of the high-tech boom may help to explain the rapid drop of demand for computers and telecom equipment.) Moreover, revisions of the national income statistics for past years and new statistics for 2000-2001 suggested that productivity growth had never been quite as fast as had earlier been thought.

As the economy reaches for a solid turnaround in 2003, the outstanding issue is whether rapid growth in the new economy will resume or whether the path taken will be the more traditional slow growth trend that has been observed for many years. Or might there even a second dip of recession? There is no denying, however, that technology and the operation and structure of business have changed significantly and are likely to continue to do so. Will these changes produce a real new economy?

Chapter 3
A Technological/ Organizational Revolution

"Productivity growth has presumably accelerated because of infor-mation technology; but promises about the rewards of such technolo-gy have been repeatedly disappointed over the past decade. Why are they finally being fulfilled now? An amateur, non-technologist's guess is that connectivity pays off in a way that mere information-process-ing does not. Replacing carbon copy memos with publication quality, laser printer reports did not add much value, but using the Internet to route trucks to the right place does. My own experience is that per-sonal computing had only a modest effect on my ability to generate and disseminate misinformation, but that e-mail and the Internet have made a big difference."[1]

Another view of the new economy is to look for changes in technology and in the structure and operation of business. From this perspective, the U.S. econo-my is undergoing a fundamental technological revolution, one that will broad-ly affect the operation and organization of businesses.

Rapid change in one sector or another might not be seen as revolutionary. Nor would gradual change extending over many years. But we may speak of a revolution when changes affect a wide range of the economy's leading sectors, when they comprehensively influence the ways in which business is organized and carried out, and when they occur within a single decade.

Even though the effects are not yet reliably apparent in the aggregate eco-nomic indicators, there is evidence that revolutionary changes are taking place in the United States economy today. We are witnessing the creation of a more

---

[1]Paul Krugman (2000) "Can America Stay on Top?" *Journal of Economic Perspectives,* 14 (1): 172.

sophisticated economy—an e-conomy. What are these changes and what is their significance?

NETWORK CONNECTIVITY

Network connectivity lies at the heart of the e-revolution. Visionaries see the network as the market in which transactions take place. The connection between computers at various levels of the business supply chain and between business and consumers has eliminated many steps that formerly required human intervention, and paperwork. Orders can now be processed automatically. The production chain can be operated efficiently, linked closely to consumer purchases at the point of sale, with optimal inventory management. You find this type of efficiency in every neighborhood at the grocery store: the scanner at the supermarket checkout counter is directly connected to company inventory files and to suppliers. Transactions and payments can be automated. Information is dispersed worldwide instantaneously—the charge you made in California can be in the billing files of your credit card company in Boston within minutes.

These new opportunities for efficiency have important implications for how business is organized. In some fields, like stock brokerage, the results have been spectacular. In many others, we are only at the beginning of a radical transformation; there is room for significant further progress revolutionizing operations broadly across the entire economy.

TECHNOLOGICAL INNOVATIONS

Technological innovations lie behind these developments. They have come at breathtaking speed in recent years, going from a couple of dozen transistors on a chip to many millions in the course of less than 20 years. There have been great increases in communications capacity and reductions in cost associated with transmitting optical signals through glass fiber cables. The speed and capacity of individual computers already allows today's small server, no bigger than a PC, to perform accounting and control functions that could be done only by a minicomputer or even a mainframe just a few years ago. The increase in speed and broadband capacity of communications is making possible rapid interaction of many computers in networks.

Investments in new computer and communications equipment and complex new software programs have been burgeoning. Here again, though there have been some spectacular results, there is still much more potential.

Finally, new software systems emerge regularly that exploit the new technology. Initial software programs, like the Visicalc spreadsheet and the dBASE data management programs, were path breaking, but they were soon superseded by more sophisticated programs, some for specialized use and some general. By and large, these were intended for operating on a separate computer or on a company's system.

The next step was the turn to network communication that allows different systems to speak to one another. Connectivity is the key, allowing specialized, sometimes proprietary, systems to communicate with each other. Java is an example of the kind of general-access communication languages that operate on today's network. The future of computer programs is increasingly in the direction of networked systems that integrate the computing power available at many nodes. And what's next?

"The competition's focus will be shifting to so-called Web services, clever software that opens the door to offering a new level of computerized automation and convenience to companies and consumers. Microsoft and its rivals, like IBM and Sun Microsystems, are scrambling to supply businesses with these services, which will allow computers to share data across the Internet and . . . handle all kinds of tasks without human intervention."[2]

The ultimate network system is still evolving. The latest enthusiasm is for creating a computer utility. To do this, two central elements must be taken into account: complexity and variations in demand. Complexity is the result of attempting to integrate systems that are, themselves, highly complex. Just the job of keeping them all up to date and in tune challenges the average business information services department. New technologies like grid computing that draw on computer capacity available at different locations make this task even more complicated.

The computer utility proposes to take on this job so that all appears seamless from the user's perspective. The demand variation dimension relates to the fact that the timing of peak loads differs. Business activity in New York reaches a peak when workers in London and Tokyo are at home. Spare capacity in one location can be used to carry out computations needed elsewhere. The potential of "computing on demand" is to give users as much capacity as they need whenever they need it. IBM has been pushing this notion hard but others—Sun, EDS, and Hewlett-Packard among them—are aiming at similar tar-

---

[2]Steve Lohr. "Microsoft is Putting Its Muscle Behind Web Programming Tools." *New York Times,* February 13, 2002.

gets. Interestingly, this turn to central management reverses the previous trend toward decentralization and replacing mainframes with small PCs.

Case 3.1
Moore's Law and Metcalfe's Law

A couple of simple rules about the progress of technology have caught the popular imagination:

Moore's Law: *The computing power of a chip is likely to increase very rapidly.* The law was named after Robert Moore, a founder of Intel, who said in 1965 that the number of transistors embedded in a chip was likely to double every 18 to 24 months. His forecast was a little on the low side. Experts predict that there is potential for continued increase at this breathtaking pace for another five or ten years. On the other hand, because it is not certain that such gains in computing power will be needed, future technical improvements may emphasize other aspects of computer technology.

Metcalfe's Law: *The more people there are on a network, the greater the value of the network to each user.* The law was named after Robert Metcalfe, a founder of 3Com, who said that the value of a network is proportional to the square of the number of users.

CHANGES IN BUSINESS PRACTICE AND ORGANIZATION

Beyond the purely technical changes associated with improved hardware and software is the question of how these developments affect practice and organization in the business world. This is where the truly revolutionary impact lies.

Consumers are only peripherally aware of the implications of computer networking through their participation in B2C, buying products on the Web, or carrying on other Web-based transactions and e-mail communication. In fact, the potential for transferring the many transactions needed along the supply chain to computer networks is enormous. Some large firms like Sears and Wal-Mart have been using computer linkages—EDI (electronic data interchange) systems—to manage production and supply for years. But theirs have been proprietary specialized systems open only to a limited number of participants. The Web opens similar systems to a vast number of potential users and promises substantial further gains in efficiency. It is possible to automate the order and delivery process and to link it closely to real time data on retail sales from point-of-sale terminals.

Changing business practices are likely to alter the organization of business. As we will see further below, changes in transaction costs and in the relationships between functional units are also likely to change the organization of business—from integrated firms to outsourcing, for example. Innovative technologies are providing opportunities for new firms to enter markets on the basis of technical advantages. Such changes are likely to be disruptive to mature organizations. At the same time, economies of scale are likely to affect the size of enterprises, giving advantages to large market-dominant organizations and to first movers. We cannot be sure precisely how the intensity of competition will be affected, but we can be sure that there will be a period of uncertainty as business practices and organizations adapt.

Ultimately, emerging IT developments promise improvements in productivity in a wide range of activities in many dimensions of the economy. But they are not being implemented without difficulty. Nor are they costless. IT investment accounts for the bulk of the increase in business fixed investment that occurred during the 1995-2001 boom.

For some firms the transition to new IT systems has been very costly indeed. Sometimes the gains in productivity associated with automatic ordering and inventory control systems have been more than offset by the cost of implementing the programs and buying the complex computer equipment and facilities required. Sometimes inability to reconcile different computer systems has made huge mergers ineffective. Sometimes the technical experts setting up the new e-businesses and IT systems have been better at computer programming than at business management. Such difficulties are inevitable when the business environment is being drastically transformed.

What makes these developments revolutionary is their breadth of their scope across the entire economy, the speed of their introduction, and, most important, the way they affect the structure and organization of business. We will be looking at the incentives for these changes in more detail in Chapter 11.

Elsewhere in the world, similar changes are becoming apparent, though there, too, the impact on aggregate statistics remains unclear. Few countries are as far advanced in e-commerce as the United States, although some are further along in selected areas, like cell phone communication. All are making progress in adapting to the new technologies. Some, like Singapore, see their future primarily in activities related to the IT revolution.

Chapter 4

Reconciling Growth and Technical Change

How do we reconcile an apparently brief record of rapid productivity growth with the evidence of rapid improvement in technology and with the e-revolution that we will consider further below? Is the new economy glass half empty or half full?

A GLASS HALF FULL

The empirical evidence is very mixed. The statistical basis for the new economy is flimsy at best, because the period of improved productivity growth was short and because it has now become obvious that the traditional business cycle was not wiped out after all.

However, there are some clear improvements over earlier periods. The 1990s represent the longest economic recovery on record, a recovery that we have related to the IT boom. This was a period with unusually low unemployment and low inflation. It was a time when the U.S. economy had strong gains in white-collar high-tech employment even as blue-collar manufacturing jobs were lost. There is not much doubt that the extended period of prosperity and growth that the U.S. economy went through in the 1990s was closely related to the technical revolution that was underway.

A positive perspective on the new economy sees it in terms not so much of measured economic performance as of technical change and opportunity. The late 1990s was a time when highly sophisticated computer equipment became a dominant part of business investment in machinery and equipment.

The gains from such innovation are typically slow to show up as increased productivity. It takes time for innovations like the PC and Internet access to be diffused widely. Though the diffusion, to be discussed in detail below, is occurring rapidly, it is far from completed. New computers and cellular telephones are being introduced more rapidly than were automobiles and electrical power early in the 20th century, for example. But more complex technical innovations, like those involved in cellular and glass fiber telecommunications and broadband Internet access, are central to the spread of e-commerce. These opportunities present technical challenges some of which have not yet been fully resolved. They, too, call for changes in business organization and operation. Implementing automated business systems at the practical commercial level is particularly challenging. The changes that are still to come may take years more to affect business efficiency.

On this basis, it is easy to argue that the glass is not half empty, it is half full (see Concluding Comment box, page 43). Enormous opportunities have been created for new e-businesses. The pipeline for innovation related to the e-business revolution is quite full. Despite the 2001 recession, prospects are bright for a resurgence of rapid technological and structural change.

GLOBALIZATION

There are close links between the IT revolution and the globalization of business. The expansion of business throughout the world, which has been going on for many years, has been one of the driving forces for economic development in many countries. Patterns of comparative advantage have been changing as manufacturing is locating increasingly in developing countries, many of which are becoming newly industrialized. High-tech IT firms remain based largely in the United States, both for hardware and software, but have transferred some of their activities, like customer service, abroad. Foreign direct investment has shifted manufacturing of many electronic products—PCs, cellular phones, flat panel displays, and disk drives—to South Korea, Taiwan, Singapore, and more recently China. In some businesses, non-U.S. enterprises dominate—Finland's Nokia in telecoms, for example.

Worldwide digital phone systems and the Internet have improved the interconnection between producing sectors in many parts of the world. Communication has become instantaneous and practically free of cost. Physical products still need to be shipped, of course, but transportation costs have been coming down. An increasingly important category, intellectual products like computer programs, TV shows, and music, and many services can be transmitted electronically and supplied from anywhere.

An interesting example of internationalization is how firms in the U.S., Israel, and India collaborate, producing computer programming in one location and transmitting it to the others. Bangalore, a technological and educational center, has become the home of the Indian programming industry. Skilled programmers can be hired there at wages that are less than one quarter of those prevailing in the United States, and a computer programming firm in Boston can transmit its requirements for programs to India in the evening and have the completed code next morning.

U.S. firms have also built programming centers in countries like Russia where high-tech engineers and programmers are widely available. Labor-intensive computational clerical activities like data input and check processing are also being sent abroad. For example, New York City tickets for environmental violations are being scanned and sent digitally for processing in Ghana.[1]

International finance relies heavily on computer connections. International financial markets are linked electronically. International dealings through financial centers like New York, London, and Frankfurt use networks to communicate not only information but also transactions.

The IT revolution is likely to further change the international division of labor. As we will note further below, some countries will gain greatly. Others may find the required transformations, improvement of education, and high-tech infrastructure almost too much of a challenge to overcome.

Concluding Comment (Part I)

- The statistical evidence of a new economy is still very inconclusive.

- While there are many changes, the underlying structure (and theory) of the economy has probably *not* changed radically.

- On the other hand, there is widespread evidence of technological progress. The tremendous gains in electronics and networks have the potential to affect business operations and organization in many fields.

- Application of the new developments is likely to lead to further rapid economic progress.

---

[1]Robert F. Worth. "In New York Tickets, Ghana Sees Orderly City." *New York Times,* July 22, 2002.

Part II
The E-Business Revolution

Chapter 5
The Essentials of E-Business

What do we mean by e-business?

Electronic commerce or e-business is the automation of commercial transactions using computers and networked communication technologies. We use the word to refer to a wide range of business activities that can be expedited or automated by the use of computer networks.

Many commercial functions have been on computers for years—bank accounts, company accounting, air transportation ticketing, and inventory control. The EDI systems used have been proprietary, specially designed, awkward, and largely for intracompany use. The revolutionary change is the introduction of the Internet, the possibility of access from all sorts of computers including PCs, and the standardization of access and operations. The Internet/World Wide Web (WWW) opens electronic connections to a wide range of participants with all kinds of systems. This has made possible B2B and B2C access.

WHAT'S E-COMMERCE ALL ABOUT?

In referring to commerce on the Internet, Jeff Bezos, founder of Amazon.com, has been quoted as saying, "There are qualitative changes so profound they become quantitative."

To most people, the most familiar aspect of e-business is ordering goods—books, computers, clothing—from a Web site. This is a type of B2C operation.

---

[1]"Now that dot-coms are no longer in fashion. . . . In a campus version of gallows humor, business school students who two years ago were hungry for jobs at Internet startups now describe B2B as 'back to banking.' B2C has suffered a similar fate: B2C is now 'back to consulting.'" *Knowledge@Wharton* (2001b). "Will Covisint Thrive as a B2B Exchange?" *<http://knowledge.wharton.upenn.edu/articles.cfm?catid=14&articleid=466>*.

Far greater potential lies, however, in B2B—transactions between businesses.[1] The dollar volume of transactions between firms, as goods move along different stages of different production and distribution channels, far exceeds GDP.

Assume you buy a shirt from XYX.com. Going all the way back to the beginning of the shirt production process, there is the production and sale of cotton and then the manufacture of the cloth, thread, buttons, trim, and packaging material. These materials are procured from many suppliers. Then, under the direction of the shirt manufacturer, the pieces are cut and the shirt is assembled, often in the Caribbean or in East Asia. Once the product is packaged, it is shipped to the distributor or wholesaler and finally to the retailer.

At each point of the supply chain, there are numerous transactions that used to involve personal communication, paperwork, billing, and payment. All that can be automated, yielding huge savings in labor costs. The process can be optimized; in the long run, the greatest savings probably result from improvements in flexibility and reductions in inventory. Many firms also claim that use of the Internet gives them a large initial reduction in the cost of their supplies because they have access to a greater range of suppliers, which intensifies competition for their business.

The business activities supported by the Internet range all the way from consumer catalogs to auction markets, supply chains, inventory management, accounting, bank accounts, even e-government. Many of the e-commerce participants have been firms new to the business, run by techies whose strength has been in computer programs and computer management. As we have noted, they have often found it difficult to learn the business aspects of the operation. Many firms have made huge investments and have yet to realize a payback. As we will see in the examples presented, few have found it easy to make profits on the Internet. In some cases, like portal and e-magazine businesses, it was never clear how revenues would be brought in. Certainly, Web advertising has turned out to be an ephemeral source of revenues. In recent years, some of the most successful firms have been conventional firms, old-fashioned bricks-and-mortar businesses, which have simply extended their activities into the e-commerce world.

Though e-business is highly competitive and dynamic, it also presents the potential for large-scale monopoly. As we will detail later, economies of scale and first-mover advantages offer the opportunity to create giant market-dominant organizations. Mergers and acquisitions have boomed as consolidation, or perhaps we should say concentration, has taken place. Dominant firms have been able to prevent the entry of newcomers and to destroy competitors. The long-run outcome of these developments, like so many other aspects of e-business, is uncertain.

NEW BUSINESS AND OLD BUSINESS COMPARED

So in what ways is the new e-business different from traditional business? The answer: In so many ways that we are often speaking of altogether different types of business.

- Many of the new e-businesses simply did not exist in the good old economy. Others represent significant improvements on traditional ways of doing things. The most obvious examples are IT hardware, software, and applications.

- Not long ago chips and glass fiber systems simply did not exist. Today, sophisticated technology based on them goes not only into advanced capital goods but also into many consumer goods, from cell phones and personal digital organizers to appliance controls and automobiles.

- The rapid shift of traditional manufacturing to less developed countries like Mexico, China, or Malaysia has meant that fewer old economy products are being manufactured in the United States and Western Europe.

- Consumers have an almost infinite number of software options for e-mail, information searches, and word processing and computation. Many of the products sold in today's market place are intellectual products, like music and videos, where the manufacturing cost is far less important that the cost of the content.

- Businesses and educational institutions have been in the forefront, using software and computers to accomplish tasks like inventory control or e-learning that had been done imperfectly before. Some traditional manufacturing firms have discovered that there is much money to be made in computer service and management—IBM now makes a larger part of its business in service areas than in manufacturing.

- E-business applies IT techniques to automating business operations. Some e-business applications are altogether new, but most of them are improvements (we hope) over existing types of business. In most cases, they make instantaneous and automatic operations that took time and human intervention in the past. Examples are stock brokerage and mail order for consumers and supply chain management for businesses. Often the new business operations supplement, but do not fully replace conventional business. At least that has been the experience so far.

- The new businesses are often in high-tech and service areas, fields where there has been much technological progress in recent years. The dynamics of growth in these areas is legendary; small firms (as Microsoft, Intel, and Dell once were) have become giants in 10 to 20 years, sometimes displacing huge manufacturing businesses. One of the biggest challenges for the next decade is to extend the era of rapid innovation by using IT techniques.

- New business fields are often, though not always, highly competitive. Technical change has been the basis for a burst of competition. With astonishing speed, new forms of communication, new computer programs, and new chips displace the old. Indeed, once a firm becomes accustomed to a particular way of doing its job, it tends to become inflexible and sticks to its existing customer base and familiar technology. This leaves openings for other enterprises following innovative paths, which may ultimately take the lead.[2]

  This phenomenon can be seen in the shift from analog to digital electronics, the move from mainframes to minicomputers to PCs, the invention of small disk drives, the introduction of the Windows operating system, and perhaps today the switch from wired to wireless services. In each case, innovators introduced new systems or products, sometimes only sophisticated modifications of the prevailing product, and displaced mature enterprises. It takes nimble footwork or a monopoly position (see Chapter 11) to remain on the leading edge in such a highly competitive world.

- Interaction between people and between firms is quite different in the new economy from what it was in the old. Where much of the contact used to be in person or over the phone, increasingly contacts are via e-mail. More important, many human contacts are eliminated altogether. Computer programs match buyers and sellers. Computer algorithms determine appropriate inventory holdings and orders are placed, often automatically, on the basis of real-time point-of-sale data. Many orders are placed and sales transacted directly on the Web site market place and are fulfilled—if the product does not require physical fulfillment—without human intervention.

---

[2]For numerous examples see Clayton M. Christenson (2000). *The Innovator's Dilemma.* New York: Harper Business.

Chapter 6
E-Commerce: B2C

B2C refers to the linkage between businesses and consumers. Computer access from the home or office to a wide variety of products gives consumers significant advantages. Instead of going to the store to choose from limited selections, consumers can let their computer mouse do the walking, picking from an almost unlimited range of products and brands on the Web. The computer itself may do the searching for the product desired; some sites actually search for the cheapest vendor. Often consumers have the convenience of "one-click shopping" and can request quick delivery.

Of course, there are disadvantages. It is not possible to handle the product, to turn it over and see how well it is made, or to try it on. There is usually a delay between the time the order goes in and the delivery. And some people miss the stimulation of going to the shopping mall.

E-RETAIL

The e-retailer faces some significant challenges. The on-line catalog must display the products fully without being so complicated as to discourage use. Some on-line catalogs give evaluations of the product, add suggestions for purchase of related products, or remember what the consumer bought the previous time. There are programs that facilitate ordering; they enter a series of products into a virtual shopping cart and easily finalize the order and payment process (check-out) without the buyer having to reenter credit card numbers.

Customized products are the latest wrinkle in e-tailing. All along, Dell has allowed its customers to select the particular combination of features they want in their computers. Now, clothing retailers have discovered that made-to-measure blue jeans command a premium price. Consumers enter their measurements and a description of their build. The information is transmitted to a cutting machine in Mexico and the finished product arrives some days later. This approach is being extended to a broad range of clothing.

Even so, some observers are beginning to question whether the on-line catalog is really much more than a mail order catalog and whether it can ever hope to get a large fraction of consumer purchasing. Some high-end retailers like Bloomingdales.com have found that customers are more likely to browse than to buy and have eliminated transactions from their Web sites. Others that sell more standard products, like *Macys.com,* continue to perform well.[1] The rapid growth of on-line shopping in general continued through 2002 despite the weakness of the economy.

The e-commerce retail market is made up of a strange mixture of firms, far from representative of normal consumer purchasing. A list of the top 25 on-line retailers is shown in Table 6.1. Dell, the leading seller of PCs, ranks first, with average purchases over $1,300, much higher than other e-retailers. Dell has been able to use the Internet to dominate the PC market (Case 6.3). Ticketmaster, next on the list of on-line retailers, sells event tickets. Consumers can search Ticketmaster's databases to ascertain the time and location of performances and the availability of tickets. Then they can order the tickets and pay for them without leaving their home computer. Amazon, number 3, is the dominant Internet bookseller but is rapidly extending its scope to other e-retail lines (Case 6.1).

It is interesting that sellers of office supplies—Office Depot, Quill, and Staples—also rank high on the e-retail list. A large share of their sales is to business office managers (note that the average sale is between $150 and $200) and often orders are from their widely distributed print catalogs rather than from Web listings. It might have been expected that electronic listings would replace the print catalog. Apparently, not so! Print catalogs seem to have a symbiotic relationship with e-retail business. This is also apparent with some other e-business retailers like Spiegel, a traditional catalog seller, although Sears has eliminated its print catalog in favor of Web listings.

Other important e-retailers are highly specialized. Quixtar uses a club plan like Amway; Victoria's Secret offers specialized clothing, FTD replaces traditional telegraph flower delivery. So far, general department stores have not made it far on the Web.

Apart from complex product listing issues, the physical, nonelectronic aspects of the transaction—the process known as *fulfillment*—have been a real challenge. This is where the young new economy entrepreneurs face old-fash-

---

[1]Bob Tedeschi. "E-Commerce Report: For a Variety of Reasons Bloomingdales.com Backs Away From Its Agreessive Internet Sales Strategy." *New York Times,* January 21, 2002.

Table 6.1: Top 25 On-line Retailers, 2001

	Market Share (%)	Average Purchase ($)	Visitors (Millions)
Dell.com	22	$1,328	12.5
Ticketmaster.com	12	159	7.8
Amazon.com	10	45	49.8
OfficeDepot.com	10	150	3.5
Quilt.com	4	159	0.4
Quixtar.com	4	126	0.7
Staples.com	3	159	2.1
Sears.com	3	282	4.3
QVC.com	3	68	1.9
OfficeMax.com	3	204	1.3
VictoriasSecret.com	2	102	2.8
SonyStyle.com	2	907	2.5
JCPenney.com	2	102	3.0
1-800-Flowers.com	2	61	2.9
TigerDirect com	2	399	1.4
Newport-News.com	2	87	1.4
HSN.com	2	90	1.7
BarnesandNoble.com	2	71	9.0
ColumbiaHouse.com	2	43	11.7
Tickets.com	2	111	1.3
Proflowers.com	1	45	2.2
FTD.com	1	67	2.0
Spiegel.com	1	177	2.0
Overstock.com	1	97	3.1
Chadwicks.com	1	91	0.9

Source: Bob Tedeshi. "E-Commerce Report: The 25 Top E-Tailers and the Various Approaches They Use–From catalogs to Handholding–to Increase Their Sales." *New York Times,* July 22, 2002.

ioned hard-core business problems. They must learn how best to manage inventories, how to fulfill the order by shipping the product, and how to handle returns—in short, how to keep the buyer happy. Many an e-retailer has been unable to meet the bricks-and-mortar challenges of the task.

Some e-retailers are fortunate in that they sell products—music and videos—that can be transmitted over the Web, but even for these products most e-retail still involves physical shipment. Electronic shipment would avoid problems of managing inventories, selecting the products ordered, packing, and transportation. It would also solve the important issue of what to do when the customer is not satisfied and wants to return the product (more about this when we discuss Napster in Case 9.1). In principle, books and videos could also be handled electronically.

In practice, we are still a long way from the 100 percent electronic transmission stage. Few people yet have the high-speed Internet connections and other equipment that makes electronic transmission practical. Delivery services like FedEx and UPS are still the biggest gainers from video-on-demand services on the Web. Copying of popular music files, with such operations as Napster and its successors, had spectacular acceptance, largely because the music was free, but the copyright holders fought back to limit access to paying customers.

In theory, a single e-retail site could serve the entire world! In practice, it remains surprisingly difficult to cross national frontiers. It is not just a matter of translating a Web site into different languages. Culture guides what people want to see on a retail Web site, what they would like to buy, and how they would like to pay. Moreover, despite the worldwide movement to reduce trade barriers, it is still difficult to ship retail products cheaply and quickly from one country to another.

While e-retailing still constitutes only a small part of total retail sales, in the fourth quarter of 2001, despite the bad economy, retail sales on the Internet surged 72 percent over the same quarter in 2000. Market researchers forecast further annual increases of nearly 30 percent over the next few years. E-retailing is clearly still a growth industry.

Case 6.1
Amazon.com

Amazon.com, the bookseller, has had a short but spectacular history. Begun in 1995, Amazon grew prodigiously, far outdistancing its traditional bookseller competitors. Its exhaustive catalog of books is easy to access and use. As in a bookstore, the prospective customer may leaf through a book, looking at selected pages. Reviews of the book and recommendations of related literature are available. It is even possible to buy used books. Anyone who has not used Amazon.com yet has undoubtedly at least heard of it.

But all has not been good in Amazonland. Huge quantities of books were being sold, but sold at a loss. Amazon has yet to make profits consistently. In some accounting reports, Amazon lost as much as 30 cents on each dollar of sales. This has happened despite the company's significant advantages:

- An enormous catalog of books—you can find anything you can think of.
- A huge scale of operation—38 million shoppers.
- An excellently designed catalog.
- A convenient shopping basket and one-stop order system.
- Overnight delivery and low prices.

So what went wrong?

Amazon began without any bricks and mortar using an outside company to fulfill its orders. When Barnes and Noble threatened to acquire Ingram, the book distributor that had fulfilled Amazon's orders, Amazon built three huge warehouses. Amazon handled the electronic transaction well enough, but it found it very difficult and costly to carry out the physical task of keeping inventories, picking the right books off the shelf, packing and shipping them, and accepting returns. The whole fulfillment function is handled most efficiently by traditional bricks-and-mortar booksellers. To simplify this process, Amazon has now made a deal with Borders to allow pickup and return of books ordered from Amazon at Borders' bookstore outlets.

In order to take advantage of its valuable and well-known Web site, Amazon expanded into many other areas—CDs, electronics, video, auctions, and toys. Because these fields were more competitive than books, Amazon found it very difficult to make any inroads on the market. Amazon also tried costly expansions into foreign markets. Finally, other booksellers, like Barnes and Noble and discounter Buy.com, have begun to catch up with Amazon.

There have been serious doubts about whether Amazon would survive, especially about whether its cash would hold out until the company became profitable. There is still a great deal of uncertainty, but so far Amazon has proved the pessimists wrong. In the last quarter of 2001, Amazon managed to squeeze out a pro forma profit—all of 1 cent per share! More important, its cash position has improved.

What changed? Amazon shifted from a "get big quick" strategy to a strategy of cutting costs and making a profit. It has reduced costs by laying off workers and closing a distribution center. In the book business, it has emphasized discounting by cutting prices and offering free shipping under certain conditions. It has expanded its portfolio of products by setting up partnerships with other retailers, like Circuit City, Toys R Us, and Target that can handle distribution directly. A "marketplace" where small businesses can sell used merchandise also accounts for a significant part of Amazon's sales. These moves could transform Amazon from an e-seller of books to an e-shopping mall. A serious question, though, is whether broadening the product line will undermine Amazon's franchise as a bookseller.

Amazon.Ca is Amazon's latest attempt to expand internationally. Even though Canada is part of NAFTA, shipment of books from the United States to Canada is sufficiently expensive to make competition difficult. Rather than setting up a physical operation in Canada, Amazon has set up a virtual business. Books ordered by Canadians on Amazon.Ca are shipped from elsewhere in Canada under contracts with local book suppliers. The Amazon.Ca Web site, designed to meet Canadian sensibilities, is operated from Seattle.

Case 6.2
E-Groceries

During the dot-com bubble, e-grocers like Webvan offered to sell groceries on the Internet and deliver to the home of the customer. It seemed like a great convenience. Not that the idea is really original, because high-end groceries have been taking telephone orders and making deliveries for decades.

When dot-coms like Webvan began to enter the business, though, they found it very difficult. The market turned out to be smaller than expected, since many consumers prefer to go to the supermarket to make their selections. Warehousing, selecting the goods ordered (picking), and delivering them turned out to be major challenges. How to pick the goods ordered efficiently? How to assure that turnover was fast enough to guarantee freshness? How to deliver efficiently? Should there be a charge for deliveries? Where should the product be left if the customer is not at home? After investing more than a billion dollars in freestanding warehouse facilities, Webvan was forced to close its doors—or, perhaps more accurately, its Web site. Its remaining assets were sold off for 10 to 15 cents on the dollar in a court-ordered auction.

Difficulties lie in the contrasts between conventional supermarkets and the requirements of Web ordering and delivery systems. Supermarkets are laid out for visual appeal. Goods are displayed so that the purchaser will be attracted not only to necessities but also to impulse items and special promotions. A similar visual approach is possible in a Web-based product display.

However, it is inefficient to source Web grocery orders directly from an existing supermarket, though some firms do that. An automated warehouse laid out for picking efficiency recognizes that some products are purchased daily and others only occasionally and allows for differences in packing and storage requirements (room temperature, chilled, or frozen) This is likely to be more efficient. But such a special warehouse needs to operate on a large scale and, once established, must be operated near full capacity. There is consequently an important trade-off between efficiency and size, one that is particularly daunting for new firms entering the e-grocery business:

"At a capacity of 8,000 orders per day, seven days per week, with an average order size of about $103, Webvan could achieve an operating margin of 12 percent compared to a 4 percent margin for a traditional supermarket. In reality, however, Webvan's distribution center operated at a loss with less than 20 percent capacity load, i.e., less than 1600 orders per day."[2]

Remaining e-grocery firms like Peapod and Tesco are associated with large traditional supermarket chains. They started out more modestly, using their existing warehouses, delivering from their retail stores, and charging for delivery. Using a store-based fulfillment model, Tesco has been able to achieve near national coverage in the United Kingdom, but operating costs tend to increase as volume of picking from store shelves rises, so Tesco, too, may find the new business challenging.

Case 6.3
Dell Computers

The *New York Times* headline on September 25, 2002 read: "On a Roll, Dell Enters Uncharted Territory." Dell has become the most successful seller of PCs and is beginning to expand into related but more sophisticated products. Started in 1984 by the 19-year-old Michael Dell from his University of Texas dorm room, the company began as a mail-order assembler and upgrader of PCs. Operating over the phone and the Internet, Dell has combined a low-cost sales and distribution model with a production cycle that begins when the order is received.

---

[2]J. Kamarainen, et al. (2001). "Cost Effectiveness in the E-Grocery Business." *International Journal of Retail and Distribution Management,* 29 (1); *<http://www.diem.hut.fi/ecomlog>*.

The central elements of its tried-and-true formula are:

- Direct sales by telephone or over the Internet.
- Direct relationships with customers, without distributors.
- Build-to-order manufacturing, though some standard models are available.
- Low spending on research and development.

The strategy of building computers to order (BTO) and selling them directly to consumers has reduced costs and minimized product inventories. As a result, consumers get precisely the products they want at a price lower than the competition charges.

In 2001, Dell sold more than 18 percent of all the PCs sold in the United States. Its shipments were rising sharply even as total industry shipments were falling. The company achieved this in part by sharply slashing prices. This has meant somewhat reduced margins but Dell has succeeded by achieving great efficiency and high volume.

Economies of scale have been augmented by computerized controls. Dell has been able to impose its own formats on its electronically controlled supply chain all the way back to equipment suppliers and logistics providers. This has been possible because computer components are highly standardized—most makes use the same memory chips and disk drives—and Dell draws on a relatively small number of suppliers. Inventories are kept to an absolute minimum; they are largely inventories of parts with almost no work-in-process or finished goods inventories, in sharp contrast to leading competitors like Compaq, Hewlett-Packard, and Gateway (see Figure 6.1).

Figure 6.1: Days of Inventory

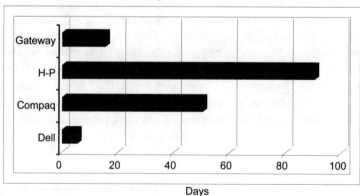

Days

Source: P. Oby. "Survey-Supply Management." *Financial Times,* June 20, 2001.

The challenge will come as Dell tries to move from PCs to more sophisticated products that call for a different marketing strategy. It is not clear that the formula that worked so successfully for PCs will do as well for Dell's planned expansion into three new markets: printers, hand-held devices, and unbranded ("white box") PCs.

These expansions may challenge the Dell business model. Printers go directly in the face of Hewlett-Packard, which controls much of the technology in this field. Unbranded PCs go to distributors, whom Dell has avoided until now. The big question is whether Dell will be able to expand into higher-margin corporate computing, with servers and related equipment. That area calls for systems integration, consulting, and services based on business practices that are quite different from Dell's current efforts.

Case 6.4
State Taxes and the Internet

Whether those who buy over the Internet should pay state and local sales taxes is a matter of considerable controversy. Under current law in the United States, states cannot tax businesses unless they have a "substantial" presence in the state. As a consequence, businesses located in one state can sell in other states without collecting local sales taxes (in principle, consumers should remit a use tax, but they do not do so).

The problems are twofold:

1. E-firms are thus favored over bricks-and-mortar firms that must collect sales taxes. The effect is a kind of subsidy.

2. Substantial revenues escape taxation. For the moment, Congress has extended the Internet tax ban, but as e-sales volume rises, it is likely to bring with it a demand, and then a means, for charging sales taxes on Internet purchases. Perhaps a general tax that will be redistributed to the states will be worked out. This is a challenge for Congress, with significant political obstacles on either side.

E-TICKETS

E-tickets are a popular e-business application. In the old system (see Figure 6.2), the traveler called the travel agent and discussed schedule possibilities. The traveler made a decision and the travel agent called again once the reservation had been confirmed. The ticket was sent along with a bill. The traveler paid the bill or submitted it to a company travel office for payment.

Figure 6.2: E-Tickets

Organization Effects: Example of E-Tickets

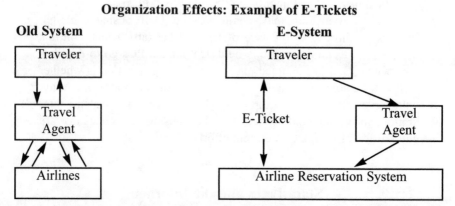

Through the Internet, travelers have direct access to airline reservations systems or to a ticketer like Travelocity or Orbitz. Many airlines offer reduced rates for booking tickets on the Web and most now impose a special charge for paper tickets. Numerous other money-saving sites offer reduced-price fares. Travelers book their own reservations directly, rather than going to the travel agent. They arrange payment through the Internet, a confirmation is e-mailed to them, and they get their boarding pass at the airport just before taking off, showing the e-mail confirmation. While it appears that all the work has been done with a few computer clicks, the traveler has taken on much of the search effort previously done by the travel agent or airline reservations personnel.

This is a good example of how Web-based transactions cause disintermediation, squeezing out the traditional intermediary. It also illustrates how new types of intermediaries based on the Web, like Travelocity, can take the place of older ones. Potentially, the travel agent can be eliminated most of the time. By saving the travel agent's commission, the airline can reduce ticket prices.

Travel agents are not necessarily cut out entirely. They still have important functions like arranging complicated travel itineraries or tours, but they now charge separately for these services.

Case 6.5
Travel Reservation Sites

The travel business is being revolutionized by a number of sites that expedite travel arrangements. Travelocity (not to be confused with Travelowcity), and Expedia are intermediaries that can book airline reservations, hotel rooms, rental cars, cruises, and related travel services. The traveler specifies the time and destination of travel and is given a menu of numerous flights that meet the required schedule. Selecting a particular flight and providing a credit card number firms up a reservation. Reservations are confirmed by e-mail and tickets are picked up at the airport just before flight time. These sites operate much like a travel agent and are paid commissions.

Some travel sites take quite a different approach. Priceline allows travelers to specify how much they are willing to pay for a particular time and destination. The traveler cannot specify an airline or a precise time of the trip. Within 15 minutes after providing the information, the prospective traveler is notified if there is a seat available at the desired price and the seat is booked. The idea is that airlines will make available seats that would otherwise go unoccupied. This is an example of the increased price competition available through the Web.

In response to these independent intermediaries, 28 airlines, led by United, Continental, Northwest, and American, have set up a jointly controlled e-market place, Orbitz. The site also books reservations for hotels and car rentals. Ticket charges are sometimes a little below the standard quoted airline ticket rate.

E-MARKETS AND E-AUCTIONS

The Internet has become a favorite location for markets and exchanges. Some of these markets are oriented directly to retail purchasers, but others deal with raw materials like energy and metals or with supplies of various kinds, spare parts, and miscellaneous other goods. E-markets are an integral part of modern supply chain management.

Some markets are organized by sellers, some by buyers, and some by intermediaries. Sellers' markets have been organized by associations of producers of raw materials. Buyers' markets are typically offered by individual or group purchasers of supplies and parts. Some automobile manufacturers attempted to organize such a market, for example. It was set up to maximize competition among suppliers and to obtain standard parts at least cost. Such markets have costs below those prevalent in the usual user/supplier relationships, but it is not yet clear that these impersonal computer market relationships can assure the same reliability and quality that have been provided by traditional business connections.

Intermediary market makers are traders not directly affiliated with either sellers or buyers. Many firms have organized commodity markets. A good example was Enron, a huge company that was the first to organize computerized markets for energy, such as natural gas and electric power, and traded actively in options and derivatives related to these products. Enron also built markets for such esoteric products as emission permits and broadband communications capacity.

The spectacular failure of Enron in 2001 probably reflects bad business practices and duplicitous accounting rather than problems with the underlying business model, but it reinforces the dictum that e-business must be guided by the same principles as conventional enterprises. Indeed, an e-company must inspire a special degree of trust, particularly when products are as ephemeral as some of the instruments that were being traded electronically by Enron.

Auction markets are one of the important uses of the Internet. Leading traditional auction houses like Sotheby's and Christie's have set up Web sites displaying goods and allowing retail customers to submit bids. Yet top-price products, like extremely rare antiques and famous art works, it appears, are still handled largely in the traditional way, with bidders present in person and by telephone at the auction house.

Among auction sellers, e-Bay is unique, as Case 6.6 demonstrates. At this site you can bid for anything from collectibles to coloring books. Most of the products are of low value, and a large number are sold by small businesses.

Case 6.6
eBay

eBay, which bills itself as the world's on-line market place, is a phenomenon. It has become America's national yard sale, and may soon be the entire world's. Based on the principle of auction sales, eBay allows individuals and small businesses to offer their goods—collectibles, cars, electronics, even clothes—for sale at auction. All transactions are handled directly between buyer and the seller; eBay is simply an electronic intermediary. eBay takes a commission on the sales and charges for miscellaneous aspects of the Web site display. Shipping and payment are left to seller and buyer to work out. Recently, eBay has opened an on-line shopping mall where firms and individuals can set up stores selling items at fixed prices. In addition to many small merchants, it has been able to attract some giant companies like Sears and Home Depot to its sales network.

Started in 1995, eBay has expanded with astonishing speed. In 1997, when computer programmer and entrepreneur Pierre Omydiar approached venture capitalist Benchmark Capital, eBay was in trouble. Though it was growing at 40 percent *per month,* it lacked professional management. Finding management talent for eBay, including CEO Meg Williams, was far more important than Benchmark's contribution to capital.

In contrast to other dot-com firms, eBay has been consistently profitable. That reflects its unique business model. According to the Financial Times, "The profit potential is huge. eBay has almost no cost of goods, no inventories, little marketing costs and no large capital expenditures.[3]

The secrets of eBay's success are:

- Its mass appeal—most of the products sold are low-cost items much like you would find at a garage sale, though some sites in the eBay mall offer more expensive products.

- Its auction format—though eBay has now added some fixed-price shopping sites.

- Its simple Web presentation—despite the vast number of items being sold, the Web site is relatively easy to use and pictures of most items are available.

- Its seller rating system—a system of stars summarizes past experiences of buyers with each vendor and vendor references are available.

- Its international scope, with sellers and buyers from all over the world.

Because eBay does not arrange shipping or payment, it avoids one of the most troublesome dimensions of e-commerce, but to facilitate the payment part of the operation, eBay has acquired PayPal, an Internet payments company. (A condition of that purchase has been that PayPal will no longer settle gambling accounts.)

eBay's lines of business and their growth rates are shown in Table 6.2. The fastest-growing area, and the one with the highest value, is sales of cars and accessories. Collectibles and art, which were the

---

[3]P. Abrahams and T. Baker. "EBay, the Flea Market That Spanned the Globe." *Financial Times,* January 11, 2002.

original mainstay and were more representative of traditional auction houses, are rapidly being replaced by "practicals."

Table 6.2: eBay's Gross Merchandise Sales, 2001

Category	Sales ($ m)	Percent of Total	Percent Change 2000-01
Autos	1,500	30	200
Computers	730	15	57
Sports equipment	670	13	33
Books, music, videos,	570	11	34
Consumer electronics	520	10	53
Photography	290	6	91
Business, office, and industrial	190	4	37
Home and garden	180	4	78
Tickets and travel	150	3	99
Clothing and accessories	140	3	126

Source: Financial Times estimates.

　　　To maintain its rapid growth, eBay has targeted foreign markets, hoping that by 2005 its business will be one-third domestic auction business, one-third domestic fixed-price business, and one-third foreign. This is an ambitious target because business in foreign countries presently amounts to only 16 percent of total revenues. eBay is hoping that its business model will click abroad as it did at home, but so far it has found the going difficult. Operations in Germany are coming along, making their first profit in 2001, and eBay is expanding in the United Kingdom, where it started from scratch, and in other European markets where it acquired other firms. But eBay has had difficulty in Japan, where Yahoo was a first mover into the auction business. Another challenge will be a move into the giant Chinese market.

Case 6.7
The Internet and Auto Sales

Automobiles represent an example of how a sector is gradually adjusting its retail operations to the Internet. On one hand there are great opportunities; on the other there are serious barriers.

Kwoka describes the following sequence:[4]

1. In the beginning, automobile Web sites performed a purely informational function, allowing computer users to find out specifications and prices of many models. These data sources supplemented print sources like *Consumer Reports.*

2. The next step was the development in the mid-1990s of referral services like Autobytel. Consumers searching for a particular vehicle would be notified what was available and would be referred to the nearest participating dealer willing to fill their request. In effect, the referral service performed the search function normally carried out by a consumer's trips to competing dealerships.

3. The next step was on-line pricing by CarsDirect as well as some of the referral services. This was more significant because it meant posting an offer price at which the car would be available. This materially changed the nature of the competition. Price was no longer a matter for one-to-one negotiation, which often permitted dealers to price-discriminate. References to the traditional manufacturer's suggested list price are no longer relevant once competitive prices are available on the Internet. The outcome is a highly competitive, usually cost-based price. (Note that dealer cost data has been available on the Internet for some time, though the figures do not take into account special dealer incentives that are often the basis for promotional pricing.)

4. On-line buying services have sprung up since 2000. A broker searches among many dealers for the specific car requested and reports where it can be obtained for the lowest price. The car is still purchased from a dealer, a legal requirement in most states, but purchasers may not even need to meet with the dealer because the car can be delivered directly to the buyer's home. Some of the Internet distributors had begun to buy dealership outlets so that they can order directly from the factory.

5. The final step is likely to be a build-to-order system. The dealer would hold little inventory. The consumer would detail the specifications of the desired vehicle, the parties would settle on a price, and only then would the car be built. In principle, the entire supply chain could be initiated at that point (see our discussion below).

---

[4]John E. Kwoka (2001). "Automobiles: The Old Economy Collides with the New." *Journal of Industrial Organization,* 19: 55-69.

The vehicle is shipped within a few days. This is very much like the system used by Dell to handle consumer PC sales.

These developments have the potential to change the automobile market drastically. The market becomes much more competitive. The role of the dealer is dramatically different. Dealers are no longer inventory holders and distributors. They become principally agents for after-sales service.

A build-to-order system may even change the nature of the whole auto production process. No longer is production planned long in advance and product pushed on the market, sometimes at a reduced price or with zero interest rate incentive schemes. Orders would now pull production in real time with minimum inventories.

The difficulty with these schemes is that their full implementation is well in the future and many consumers will continue to buy cars from local dealers as they have in the past. So far, while a large number of prospective auto purchasers go e-window shopping, only a minute fraction buy their cars directly through the Internet.

Chapter 7
E-Commerce: Supply Chain Management

Although actual and potential productivity gains from the networked economy have been associated widely with high-tech electronics firms and with the newest of new economy enterprises, the dot-coms, the greatest payoffs for the economy as a whole will occur when the old sectors of the economy take full advantage of the new opportunities. This applies particularly to the complex linkages that tie old economy manufacturers like those in the auto industry with the myriad producers of parts and other supplies.

Figure 7.1 shows a simplified picture of the supply chain from raw materials through assembly and distribution to the retail level of the assembled product. The product is assembled (middle of the figure) from parts secured from a number of suppliers, who in turn draw on numerous vendors of raw materials. Once the product has been assembled, it goes to wholesalers who in turn distribute it to the retailers.

In the supply chain there are an extraordinary number of transactions and interactions with suppliers and distributors. Firms must solicit bids, settle on prices and quantities, and schedule and track shipments, all while controlling inventory. Billing and payment entail another complex set of operations, as do various aspects of accounting. Many of these operations have gradually been shifted from personal interaction and multiple carbon copy paper to computers. The target is to integrate the entire supply chain management process on one computer network, reaching from the point-of-sale terminal through the manufacturer to the supplier.

Technological innovations in Internet and intranet communication have dramatically reduced the costs of building and operating supply chains. Computer-based procurement and on-line markets reduce procurement time and make deliveries more predictable. This cuts requirements for inventories and losses of perishable products and greatly reduces, as we have noted, the direct costs of order processing and verification. On the other hand, building and operating such supply chains still present important challenges. That these problems are much better handled by some firms than by others is apparent from the success of Wal-Mart and the failure of K-Mart.

Figure 7.1: The Supply Chain: Material and Product Flows

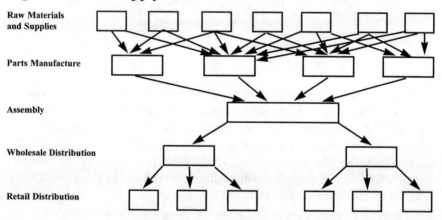

An increasing number of supply chain operations are being carried out by independent logistics companies. These manage the flow of materials through an organization from raw materials to finished products. The business is becoming increasingly complex as new technology and greater use of the Internet open new ways of passing around information, which in turn is forcing the freight transport industry to reshape and consolidate. FedEx, UPS, and DPWN (Deutsche Post) have been leaders, but a number of other companies offer more specialized services.

The Economist provides an interesting example:

> *"So what exactly can smart logistics do for companies? One example is TPG's contract with Ford. TPG has to organize 800 deliveries a day from 300 different parts makers. The software must be tied into Ford's computerized production system. Loads have to arrive at 12 different points along the assembly lines without ever being more than 10 minutes late. Parts must be loaded on trucks in a pre-arranged sequence to speed unloading at the assembly line. To make all this run like clockwork takes a team of 10 computer-wielding operations planners and two hundred unskilled workers."[1]*

---

[1] "A Moving Story." *The Economist,* December 7, 2002.

Where could this trend lead? The logistics operators may eventually organize everything except product development, design, and marketing. Along the supply chain, freight companies increasingly do packaging, labeling, and some manufacturing. In consumer electronics the growth of contract manufacturing, often organized by logistics companies, may eventually account for a substantial share of production.

Case 7.1
Supply Chain Management in the Automobile Industry

The auto industry is an extreme example of the complexity of supply chains. It is an old sector that is gradually adapting to the new economy. In this industry, the potential for saving is very large—an estimated $1,500 or more per car produced.

The auto manufacturer must schedule production, contract with suppliers, and arrange for shipment of components and parts. In the past this involved, first, forecasting and scheduling production of different models of cars, variously equipped, for the coming model year. Forecasts were based on estimates of demand and schedules were designed to keep plants running efficiently, hopefully near capacity. Components like engines and transmissions were produced in specialized plants and shipped as required to the assembly plants. Thousands of different parts had to be secured, either from company-owned parts plants or from outside suppliers who competed for the company's business This required an enormous amount of management effort: planning, scheduling, communication, setting product and parts specifications, bargaining, scheduling production and shipping, verifying, etc.

The many transactions with suppliers were carried out by specialized personnel. When the production schedule required, or when inventories ran low, the operating department sent an order to the purchasing department. Someone there negotiated with potential suppliers on price, specification, and delivery. The supplies were ordered, payments were made, and the supplies delivered.[2] Substantial inventories of parts and goods in process were necessary to avoid the possibility of running out of parts critical to the smooth functioning of the assembly line.

To summarize:

1. An enormous amount of communication and negotiation was formerly needed, first to determine specifications and prices of the

---

[2]John E. Kwoka (2001). "Automobiles: The Old Economy Collides with the New." *Journal of Industrial Organization,* 19: 55-69.

inputs, and then to supply the quantities of product required to meet retail demand. Billing and payment also involved considerable repetitive effort.

2. Inventories had to be kept at each level in order to provide flexibility. Firms want to reduce inventories to the smallest quantities possible, but if inventories are too low, or cannot be replenished quickly enough, there is danger of a stockout disrupting the entire production chain. "Just-in-time" inventory management allows firms to get along with greatly reduced stocks of parts; it is facilitated by computerization of the inventory management process and by network communication with suppliers.

3. Increased competition among an expanded number of potential suppliers whose bids can be solicited over computer networks has often reduced prices of material inputs.

The development first of EDI in the early 1990s and then of the Internet a few years later made it possible to carry out supply chain transactions electronically, sometimes even automatically. The appearance on the Internet of on-line exchanges (to be discussed further below) was the next change in the automation of supply chain relationships. In the new electronic supply chain world, there is little or no need for personal interaction or paperwork. Because transaction costs are reduced, deliveries can be scheduled more often and for smaller lots. All this made it possible for firms to adopt more flexible production and just-in-time inventory systems.

According to John Kwoka, an economist at Northeastern University:

"Over the next decade the traditional model of the auto business is likely to be substantially replaced by an Internet-based manufacturing system together with a car-ordering system that alters the role of dealers. Ultimately, these may be integrated into an electronic built-to-order system connecting individual buyers and auto parts suppliers so that the consumer's choice can be produced and delivered to his door within days."[3]

---

[3]Ibid., p. 55.

Case 7.2
Cisco Systems

Cisco Systems is the major provider of network solutions for transporting data, voice, and video. It sells routers, switches, and various access products particularly to the telecom industry. The company is a recognized leader in managing business electronically, using integrated computer systems to project demand and input requirements and control relationships with customers and suppliers through Internet and intranet connections. It became known not only for its consistently rapid growth, averaging 70 percent annually, but also for its elaborate electronic information systems that supposedly gave managers real-time access to operating data and enabled Cisco to close its books in less than one day ("virtual close" software).

According to *Business Week:*

"At the height of the Internet frenzy, it was the very embodiment of the age. When it came to Cisco, everything seemed faster, bigger, and better. Its sales and earnings growth were second to none. It sold more sophisticated gear over the Internet than any other company as it raced to fill a demand that seemed unquenchable . . . . For one brief, heady moment, it became the most valuable corporation on the planet."[4]

With its sophisticated e-management, Cisco might have been expected to avoid miscalculations of demand and schedule production precisely to minimize inventories. There would be no earnings surprises. Unfortunately, things did not happen that way.

In 2001, Cisco was caught unawares by the collapse of equipment orders from telecom firms. The result was a mountain of excess inventories of both parts and finished products. Worse, this happened in a world where technical change is so rapid that today's product is tomorrow's antique; inventories of last year's product are often worthless. Cisco had to take over $2 billion in write-offs. As many smaller telecoms that had ordered equipment went broke, the Cisco order book dropped precipitously. Meanwhile, many Cisco products became available on the gray market (some on eBay) at a fraction of their original prices.

Some economists have argued that with real time IT-based production controls, businesses would never have excess inventories, a fact that, if true, would help to wipe out the business cycle. The case of Cisco and many other IT hardware and telecom firms that found

---

[4]"Cisco: Behind the Hype." *Business Week,* January 21, 2002.

themselves with excess inventories in 2001 shows how even the most sophisticated inventory management can go awry.

Part of the Cisco myth was founded on the super-sophisticated electronic systems that were supposed to use the Internet to link Cisco to its suppliers and contract manufacturers. Instead, this system may have been the source of the difficulty, because it failed to anticipate the unexpected drop-off in demand for equipment that occurred in late 2000 and early 2001. As a trade magazine said, "The poster company for the new economy not only failed to anticipate the economic downturn, its much-heralded forecasting software and outsourcing infrastructure may have even made things worse."[5]

In 2000, when new orders were coming into Cisco at unsustainable rates and supply shortages were developing, no one stopped to ask the right questions. The automated demand forecasting system moved along with no human intervention. The system uses complex statistical procedures to combine reports from sales representatives with recent historical trends. It has little room for macroeconomic inputs or judgmental appraisals. Were the orders reported realistic? Or did customers order more than they needed to improve their chances of getting deliveries in the face of long lead times? How long could total product demand continue to expand at that extraordinary rate? When demand suddenly slowed dramatically and orders evaporated, Cisco got stuck with parts and components already ordered or in inventory. Hence the massive write-offs. Even the best real-time technology does not guarantee protection—though it should be noted that Cisco's less automated competitors, Lucent and Nortel, found themselves in even worse shape.

The consensus is that Cisco's vaunted systems were not as accurate and consistent as had been suggested. It is easy to forecast accurately when demand is going only one way, up. When that has been happening for some time, though, it is very difficult to predict turning points and to pass information about that down the supply chain. More macroeconomic information and better evaluation of uncertainties might have helped. There is no way to know.

Cisco has since added new checks and balances. It passes information about its estimates of future demand to contract manufacturers and suppliers to keep them on the same wavelength. It now checks its regional and product forecasts against surveys and other external information.

---

[5]"What Went Wrong with Cisco?" *CIO Magazine,* January 8, 2001; <*http://www.cio.com/archive/080101/cisco_content.html*>.

Questions have also been raised about Cisco's accounting, which was known to be aggressive. Its pro forma earnings were much higher than actual earnings after allowing for write-offs—and there were many such reductions because the value of many of Cisco's acquisitions failed to meet expectations. One study by Harvard's Michael Porter determined that is was impossible to tell how much profit Cisco really made in the 1990s.[6]

After the drastic decline that accompanied the pricking of the telecom bubble, in early 2002 Cisco CEO John Chambers predicted annual growth of at least 30 percent a year, but most analysts were skeptical.

B2B EXCHANGES

B2B exchanges play a crucial role in supply procurement. It was expected at the outset that independent public exchanges would dominate this field, but these are increasingly being replaced by exchanges operated by industry consortia, like Covisint in the automobile industry or by private single-company procurement operations. Observers see these developments as evolutionary rather than revolutionary, reinforcing rather than simply replacing traditional ways of dealing with suppliers.

Internet exchanges have the potential to greatly reduce the costs of information and coordination. Automating the procurement process may reduce costs per auto parts purchase from $75-$150 down to the $10-$30 range.[7] They also facilitate communication and collaborative planning and design. Finally, they introduce the concept of auctions into relationships with suppliers. That makes the procurement process more competitive and may reduce costs.

On the other hand, Internet exchanges depersonalize the relationship with suppliers and may reduce trust and collaboration. Clearly, public exchange systems are more feasible for standardized products than for supplies that are more specialized or even customized.

In addition to the consortium in the auto industry, other procurement consortia include:

- Worldwide Retail Exchange, used by major multinational retailers.
- Transora, for major food suppliers.
- Metalspectrum, a marketplace backed by leading metals companies.

---

[6]Michael Porter. "Strategy and the Internet." *Harvard Business Review,* March 2001. *<http://harvardbusinessonline.hbsp.harvard.edu/b01/en/common/item_detail.jhtlm?id=6358>.*
[7]"The Evolution of B2B: Lessons from the Auto Industry" *Knowledge@Wharton* (2001); *<http://knowledge.wharton.upenn.edu/articles.cfm?catid=14&articleid=466>.*

- Pantellos, a consortium of energy and utility companies.

Private B2B systems are also being installed, interestingly, even by auto companies that are already members of Covisint. The role of public exchanges may ultimately be to help buyers and sellers find each other. The actual supply chain transactions, which must be repeated again and again over long time periods, may be done over private networks, where it may be easier to optimize logistics and safer to transmit proprietary information.

Case 7.3
Covisint

In 1999, Ford and General Motors began on-line supply exchanges to serve as the interface between the companies and their suppliers. For contract business, suppliers would make arrangements about prices and deliveries on-line. Wherever possible, supply needs would be put up for bid, using a reverse auction method to set prices. The hope was that costs of parts would be bid down by widened competition. The Internet would also be used to manage the contracts and the billing and production scheduling, greatly reducing these management costs.

Suppliers were not pleased about having to join a number of separate Internet supply systems (one for each auto producer) that might have different standards and procedures. To deal with this problem, the auto firms created a pioneering joint venture, Covisint. Started in 2000 by industry giants Daimler Chrysler, Ford, General Motors, Nissan, and Renault, Covisint was to be a B2B supplier exchange. Covisint presents a standardized computer network environment within which suppliers can interact with their auto industry customers and with each other. Security is an essential ingredient so that each firm's information and negotiations are kept confidential from other participants.[8]

In the old industry, there were diverse standards and duplicate framework program efforts for each independent auto producer. Covisint proposes common standards and a common program platform. Presumably, this will lead to greater efficiency and reduced costs for both suppliers and manufacturers.

It is too soon to judge whether the promise of Covisint will be fulfilled. It is likely that the auto companies will continue to do a significant part of their buying separately. Exchanges are, of course, best suited for dealing in standardized products, but in the auto industry,

---

[8]A graphic description of the Covisint business diagram can be found from Covisint's Web site at *<http://www.covisint.com/solutions/corp/res/portal_diagram.gif>*.

parts have been getting more complex and unique as the companies increasingly outsource entire assemblies rather than single pieces. This means, paradoxically, that exchanges are becoming a less suitable way to handle auto industry supply relationships.

Moreover, there are some important concerns about their effect on competition.[9] While exchanges do widen the scope of competition on the supplier side, a joint auto industry exchange increases the possibility of collusion, whether tacit or explicit, among the purchasers (and possibly also among suppliers). The companies may find out what other firms are buying, and at what prices. The suppliers may get together to produce standardized inputs. Though the Federal Trade Commission gave tentative clearance to Covisint, it indicated that it will monitor its impact on competition.

Case 7.4
An Alphabet Soup of IT Businesses and Experiences

Computer applications specialists speak a jargon of their own. The following are some of the newest terms, to give some idea of the broad range of network computing:

- CRM, customer relationship management, a field in which Seibel Systems is a leader.
- ECR, efficient consumer response systems, linking point-of-sale data to suppliers.
- ERP, enterprise resource planning.
- ERM, employee relationship management.
- EAI, enterprise applications integration, which allows all applications to communicate with each other.
- 3PL, third-party logistic supplier.
- LIMS, laboratory information management system.

An essential ingredient in most of these B2B or intranet operations is integration of many programs, each designed initially for an altogether different specialized purpose. While this often represents an enormous challenge, building and installing a new comprehensive integrated system that would accomplish all the different tasks would be even more costly.

---

[9]*Knowledge@Wharton* (2001b).

Here are some comments about these types of system from young engineers participating in a part-time MBA program:

"As a user of XYZ, I only see a very small portion of all XYZ functions. I could have used more if I knew of the existence of the other functions and how to use them. This is a typical problem for many e-business end users."

"Over the last four years, I have worked as a consultant for several Fortune 500 pharmaceutical and start-up biotech companies in the U.S., Canada, and Puerto Rico. . . . Most of the laboratories still use paper-based systems, mainframes running VAX/VMS or AS400 systems, or legacy client/server applications that are several versions behind current software technology. Most of these companies attempted to migrate to client/server applications but the failure rate was high and many went back to paper-based systems. Web-based applications were not even a consideration since there were not available. It would take almost two years to implement a simple laboratory information management system (LIMS)."

The author goes on to say that one of the difficulties has been the need to keep documentation for the Food and Drug Administration. Another engineer commented:

"The direct application of e-business methodologies in contracting and service delivery is not common in the consulting industry. The complexity of typical assignments, degree of professional skill required, and need for interpersonal relationships between client and consultant generally preclude the negotiation of contracts and direct sale over the Internet."

On the other hand, an engineer writes about a chip design company:

"By using the Internet to exchange all designs within a concurrent environment with wafer manufacturers, process developers, component assemblers, and test suppliers, a start-up company of less than 15 individuals can design, qualify, and mass-produce a complex integrated circuit in approximately 18 months. A decade ago, this process would have been very labor-intensive to develop, plan, coordinate, schedule, produce, and ship, etc. The development cycle for such an integrated circuit would have been 24 to 30 months for even a large semiconductor manufacturer not too long ago."

Chapter 8
Financial Services: E-Brokerage and E-Banking

Many financial service businesses have taken advantage of Web-based operations, but the legacy of extensive systems like the banks' internal computer accounting systems and ATMs has been a barrier to rapid adoption of e-commerce in consumer banking.

E-BROKERAGE

E-brokerage is the new economy's success story. As late as the mid-1990s there were no e-brokerages. Today more than half of all consumer stock brokerage is done electronically. This has enormously reduced costs from the traditional way of investing in stocks and bonds by calling up your friendly broker, but with the reduction in cost has come a loss of personal contact between customers and brokers. Nevertheless, for the economy as a whole, the gains in efficiency are tremendous: a much higher trading volume is being accomplished with fewer workers.

While the new Web-based e-brokerage firms have been competing successfully with conventional brokers, other aspects of the securities business have not gone electronic as quickly.

The basic tasks that need to be carried out here fall into three classes:

1. Providing information on stock prices, graphs, data on firm performance, etc.

2. Managing individual stock brokerage accounts.

3. Matching buyers and sellers and establishing the market price for each security.

Note there is no physical fulfillment function here; everything can be carried out electronically. The stock certificate has gone the way of the dodo bird.

The informational and the account management functions of brokerage firms have gone a long way toward complete electronic automation. The amount of data available to investors through the Internet is almost without limit: current stock prices, past performance, charts, option chains, evaluation by stock analysts, profit projections. The only thing missing is the advice of a friendly broker.

Most Internet brokerage accounts provide direct links to the various kinds of information investors want, as well as detailed up-to-the-minute information on each investor's account position. Stock can be bought or sold with a click of the mouse. Most computerized brokerages continued to provide printed transaction confirmations on paper but it is only a matter of time until these confirmations are phased out. E-brokerage accounts have been meeting a need.

The function of stock exchanges is to establish equilibrium prices for securities, setting prices that will bring supply in line with demand. Traditionally, this work has been carried out by traders operating on the exchange floor who take orders to buy and to sell. For most securities, there are specialists who make a small margin on each transaction by matching buyers and sellers. While the records of the exchanges have been kept on computers for many years, transactions on most exchanges still require human interaction.

Electronic exchanges are a new development. They can handle transactions entirely electronically, matching a list of buyers at various prices with a corresponding list of sellers and closing the transactions automatically. Some smaller markets have gone fully electronic, matching all their buyers and sellers on the computer. Large markets like the New York Stock Exchange (NYSE) still fall short electronically; their full automation is still some time in the future.

Managing an e-brokerage operation is not a bowl of cherries. Vast amounts of money must be handled and the security of the account holder must be guaranteed. Here no mistakes are permitted; the computer system must be 100 percent reliable. Another challenge is in the area of financial advice. Though there is lots of financial information on the Web, many investors prefer the hand-holding and advice that only a human account executive can provide.

An interesting question is whether the behavior of markets has changed as a result of widespread cheap access to Web-based stock exchange transactions. The explosion of day trading in recent years may well have been a result. While day trading has just about disappeared, the volume of transactions today is far greater than in the old pre e-brokerage days. But it is not certain what impact access to the Web may have had on the trend or volatility of markets.

Case 8.1
Web-based Brokerage Accounts

E-brokerage began with discount brokers like Charles Schwab, though some e-brokers began entirely as Web-based operations, notably E*trade. Investment firms like Fidelity and conventional brokerage houses like Merrill Lynch have been forced to follow them into Web-based systems, though they stand to lose brokerage revenues.

E-brokerage has been successful enough that almost half of all stock market transactions are now carried out on the Internet. Why? There are a number of good reasons that help to explain the success:

- The costs of buying and selling stocks and bonds using an Internet account are far lower than the costs of trade using conventional brokers. It is possible to buy or sell substantial blocks of stock for fees as low as $9.99.

- It is easy to open an Internet account and the operations are user-friendly.

- Extensive information is readily accessible on the Internet.

- Internet trading is fast and efficient not only for stocks but also for options and other derivatives.

The result has been a rise in trading volume, and many new traders, mostly amateur and some day trading. This is what has caused the concern that volatility has increased and that speculative swings could threaten the stability of the financial system.

E-BANKING AND PAYMENT SYSTEMS

The headline read "E-Banking, Where Art Thou?" and the story went on: "It would appear that Mr. and Mrs. America are going to need a gentle push if the on-line banking industry is to take off."[1] Internet banking and payments systems are just not as far along as e-brokerage.

Banks have used EDI computer systems for years for their bookkeeping and for their ATMs, but the systems were internal and company-specific. They were not directly accessible to depositors or borrowers. Today, though Internet banking is widely available, consumers do not use it extensively—less than 1 percent of banking transactions in 2002 were Web-based. Why this is so is any-

---

[1]*E-Commerce Times,* February 22, 2000, at *<http://www.newsfactor.com/perl/printer/6266>.*

one's guess. On-line customers have evidently decided that PC banking is not easy, is not safe, or does not provide a significant cost saving. For many people, it is just not worth the trouble.

There remain a number of possibilities for e-banking activities through electronic delivery of traditional products:

• Checking account balances.

• Transferring funds.

• Applying for loans.

These are the types of banking activities that would be carried out at the teller's window or at the ATM. But there is no possibility of withdrawing cash or of depositing paper checks on the Web.

There are also a number of new banking products that are naturally Web-based:

• Electronic bill payment.

• Electronic money and electronic checks.

• Purchase of securities and insurance.

Banks have been trying to extend their activities. Using electronic means they can go into brokerage transactions or insurance, activities that would previously have required a staff of trained people. Ultimately, the objective is to integrate the ATM, on-line banking, and other banking functions.

On-line banking would provide substantial cost savings. Sun Trust Banks reports that the cost of an on-line transaction is about 1 cent, of a phone transaction 5 cents, and of a transaction with a teller at a bank branch $1 to $2.

The extension of bank operations onto the Internet does pose some strategic and some practical risks.

Strategically, the question is how to integrate the Internet operation with the traditional banking system, thereby reducing costs (hopefully) without losing revenues. Which products should be provided electronically? How should electronic operations be integrated with branch banks and ATMs?

Operational risks are also a concern. For one thing, banking must be 100 percent reliable. For another, as with much other e-commerce and finance, there are always questions of privacy and security. Can e-banks assure secure and confidential accounting and financial operations?

Electronic billing is a convenience that banks often provide on-line, but it is also available from free-standing billing companies. The basic idea is to eliminate bills and checks sent by mail. Payments are made from a central billing site. The U.S. Postal Service offers a bill payment system. Paypal.com allows members to make a payment to anyone who has an e-mail address. A large part of its volume represents payments for eBay auction transactions— eBay has recently acquired Paypal.

Figure 8.1 is a simplified representation of an e-billing system. At the end of the month the biller, say your electric company, automatically sends the bills to the bill settlement Web site. The latter notifies consumers, who click to indicate their agreement to pay. In turn the bill settlement site notifies the biller's bank, which collects from the consumer's bank account. The savings for the consumer are in no longer having to send a payment by mail and for the creditor in no longer having to bill and to receive and process the customer's check.

Figure 8.1: E-Billing System

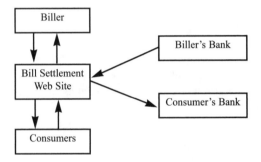

Case 8.2
Internet Banking at Citigroup

Citigroup has been a leader in e-banking. It has a broad strategy of offering a wide range of e-banking products for both businesses and consumers. Despite its massive branch banking network, Citi seeks to enlarge its customer base by offering personal and corporate bank accounts electronically. This strategy is intended to counter pure Internet banks. After very large investments in a free-standing e-Citi operation, the Citigroup merged its independent on-line banking operations into Citibank On-line, part of its consumer and business banking group. The on-line operation provides all standard deposit and loan banking services, plus brokerage and on-line bill payment.

Citi has also added MyCiti, an account aggregation service that collects information from all a client's accounts at Citi and elsewhere. Commercial and savings accounts, brokerage accounts, retirement accounts, credit card balances, even frequent flyer mile accounts show on a single page. So far, this service is free, even for people who do not bank at Citibank.

MyCiti has done far better than its developers expected. Clearly, Citigroup hopes that users will begin to ask for other Citi services so that Citi can target them for services like its mutual funds sales, its person-to-person payments system (C2it), student loans, and mortgage and home equity loan services (myhomeequity.com). Moreover, the MyCiti accounts are a spectacular source of data on each participant's financial situation, a goldmine of information that can help Citi target its promotional activities.[2]

Two critical issues for the consumer are the bother of setting up an on-line account and the question of costs. (In my own experience, it took three visits to my local branch to add the bill-paying feature to my on-line account.) The cost savings from banking on the Web are far smaller than in Web-based stock brokerage transactions. Fees vary; it is notable that though bill payment services at Citi are free on the Internet, there is now a fee for personal service. Some other banks impose monthly charges for on-line bank account services.

Most on-line banking operations are simply appendages of existing brick-and-mortar banks, though pure Internet banks like Netbank have been available for some years. They have not had great success at luring customers away from conventional banks.

While on-line banking can offer banks significant savings on transaction costs, the technology is easily replicated by competitors. For the brick-and-mortar banks, on-line banking service is likely to remain a cost reduction or a defensive strategy rather than a profit center because initial costs are high and profit margins likely to be thin. Studies have shown, however, that the option of PC banking may be a way of retaining high-profit customers, those who are more likely to extend their use of the on-line banking facility into other business with the bank, such as investments.

---

[2] *<http://www.darwinmag.com/read/100101/dime_content.html>*.

Chapter 9
Other E-Commerce Activities

A broad range of other commercial activities are potentially e-based, those that could gain significant advantage by relying on open networked computer connections. We are all familiar with e-mail and with job and real estate listings, but few are aware of the broad uses made of computers and the Internet in engineering and car design; keeping track of enrollments, grades, and credits at universities; weather forecasting, market research studies based on real-time purchasing information; and personnel management, among many other activities. Some of these are already highly developed. Others are still in early stages. The potentials in this field are still wide open. A sampling of e-business activities is summarized in Table 9.1. The potential uses of networked computer power go far beyond conventional business; there are also vast opportunities in government, health care, and education.

Table 9.1: The Range of E-Business Activities

- E-mail.
- Portals and search engines.
- E-music.
- E-zines.
- E-books.
- E-want ads (including personals).
- E-labor markets.
- E- photo processing.
- E-health care.
- E-government.
- E-learning.

An unfortunate fact is that e-pornography and e-gambling have become massive and largely uncontrolled e-businesses. The international scope of these activities is remarkable; sites located on the other side of the world—the Isle of Man is a favorite base for e-casinos—often compete as equals with domestic purveyors.

An alternate way of looking at the Internet economy is summarized in Table 9.2, where Internet business is classified into four layers. The classification was used as a basis for estimating the size of the Internet economy: approximately $300 billion, 1.3 million workers, giving an output of $250,000 per worker. The latest figures are for 1998; the sector may well have more than doubled in size since then. Note that the calculation only covers the soft parts of Internet-related operations, omitting the hardware.

Table 9.2: Layers of the Internet Economy

Layer 1: Internet Infrastructure

In this layer are companies with products and services that help create an IT-based network infrastructure, a prerequisite for electronic commerce.

- Internet backbone providers (Quest, Worldcom).
- Internet service providers (Mindspring, AOL, Earthlink).
- Networking hardware and software companies (Cisco, Lucent, 3Com).
- PC and server manufacturers (Dell, Compaq, Hewlett-Packard).
- Security vendors (Accent, Checkpoint, Network Associates).
- Fiberoptics makers (Corning).

Layer 2: Internet Applications

Products and services in this layer build on the network infrastructure and make it technologically feasible to perform business activities on-line.

- Internet consultants (US Web/CKS, Scient).
- Internet commerce applications (Netscape, Microsoft, IBM, Sun).
- Multimedia applications (RealNetworks, Macromedia).
- Web development software (Adobe, NetObjects, Allaire, Vignetter).
- Search engine software (Inktomi, Verity).
- On-line training (Sylvan, Prometric, Assymetryx).
- Web-enabled data bases (Oracle, IBM, Microsoft, SQI, Server).

Layer 3: Internet Intermediaries

Internet intermediaries increase the efficiency of electronic markets by facilitating the interaction of buyers and sellers on the Internet. They act as catalysts in the process through which investments in the infrastructure and application layers are transformed into business transactions.

- Market makers and vertical industries (VerticalNet, PCOrder).
- On-line travel agents (TravelWeb, 1Travel).
- On-line brokerages (E*Trade, Schwab, DLJDirect).
- Content aggregators (Cnet, ZDnet, Broadcast).
- Internet ad brokers (Doubleclick, 24/7 Media).
- On-line advertising (Yahoo, ESPN, Sportzone).

Layer 4: Internet Commerce

Internet commerce is the sales of products and services to consumers and businesses over the Internet.

- E-tailers (Amazon, Sears, Staples).
- Manufacturers selling on-line (Cisco, Dell, IBM).
- Fee/subscription-based companies (thestreet, WSJ).
- Airlines selling tickets on-line (UAL, AA, Delta, Orbitz, Expedia).
- On-line entertainment and professional services.

Source: A study of "The Internet Economy Indicators" done by the University of Texas and sponsored by Cisco; *<http://www.Internetindicators.com/indicators.html>*.

This classification suggests that consumers see only the tip of the iceberg of the e-conomy. Layers 1 and 2, which provide infrastructure and software applications, account for about half the revenue and the employment in the field. The part that relates directly to the sale of goods and services to consumers and business, Layers 3 and 4, accounts for the other half, though as e-business expands, the share attributable to Layers 3 and 4 is likely to grow.

Some points about e-business activities that have not been discussed earlier are appropriate here:

- **E-mail.** In a very short time, e-mail has become the major means of communication for many consumers and businesses. The degree of connectivity provided at little or no cost is not only astonishing, it is greatly appreciated by most users, especially (I suppose) by people who have developed friendships on line. But its principal economic significance lies in the fact that it has greatly accelerated and reduced the cost of business correspondence. E-mail has been expanded to allow transmission of attachments including not just pictures but also video and audio. For many people, e-mail services are free or are provided by their employers. Many others subscribe to AOL, MSN, and similar providers (ISPs) that give them other services in addition to e-mail.

- **Portals.** These sites were among the earliest Web-based utilities to be widely accepted by consumers. To begin with, they were used principally to search for information and were judged by the effectiveness of their search engines. To gain traffic they added many other services, like e-mail, guides to Internet content, news, stock market data, chat rooms, and classified ads.

  Today, broad portals are more than on-line gateways allowing the user to access many different services; "they have become destinations of content, commerce, and community."[1] Portals are an important component of activity on the Web, since as many as 60 percent of user sessions include a visit to a portal, but it has been difficult for services like Yahoo that are largely free to users to find a way to make money. Some portals like AOL charge subscription fees. Free services are gradually diminishing.

  The typical portal business model seeks revenues not only from subscriptions but also from transaction fees, referrals, licensing fees, and advertising. Figure 9.1 shows Yahoo's diverse sources of revenue. Though on-line advertising was expected to be a principal source of revenues, it has not grown as expected, and already pop-up ads have become a nuisance to many users. "Pay per click," where advertisers pay only in relation to the number of times users click on their sites is a unique way to charge for Web advertising. Revenues are also obtained by charging companies to be listed in search engine results.

  Most search engines, including AOL and MSN, have made deals with Overture, which auctions off the rights for preferential positioning on the computer search result screen. Some firms sell products directly over the Internet or host Internet shops. Some sell services, like extra e-mail storage. Yahoo has recently expanded into classified advertising and job listings with Hotjobs.com. Features like instant messaging and photo processing have been added.

---

[1]Fernando Robles (2002). "The Evolution of Global Portal Strategy." *Thunderbird International Business Review*, I: 25-47.

Figure 9.1: Yahoo Gross Revenue, 2001

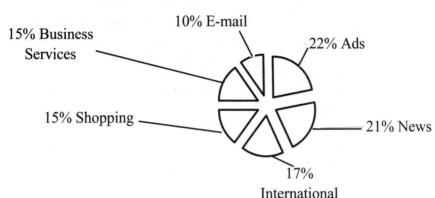

Source: Saul Hansell. "Mr. Semel's Internet Search: How a Former Hollywood Man is Trying to Make Yahoo Click." *New York Times,* January 7, 2002.

AOL, the biggest Internet service provider and portal, has been having troubles all its own. The merger with Time Warner that was supposed to provide content failed to boost growth as expected. A new strategy calls for emphasizing extra charges for broadband communication, new premium content offerings, and a discount shopping site. The question being raised is whether AOL will become a broad e-commerce vendor; in other words, will AOL become Amazon.com?

For consumers, information search has been one of the most spectacular benefits of the Internet. As *Newsweek* said, "Google has become a high tech version of the Oracle of Delphi. . . . To google something has become a verb."[2] This master source of all information is free to users. How does it make money? By licensing its services to the portals (AOL and Yahoo), by allowing corporations to use its system to sort through private data, and, most important, by selling advertising—though Google is careful not to mix its information files and advertising, which appears separately on the right of the computer screen. The question has been raised whether ultimately Google will want to become a portal with its own content and communications services.

In view of the worldwide connectivity provided by the Web, replication in other countries of services already familiar in the U.S., thus creating a global portal, represents an obvious portal expansion strategy. While the major portals have operations in many countries (AOL in 17 countries, Yahoo in 27, and MSN in 31), competition from local

---

[2]Steven Levy. "The World According to Google." *Newsweek,* December 16, 2002.

portals has been challenging because of the varied conditions in different countries. Markets differ greatly. In Japan wireless access dominates—DoCoMo's i-mode Internet access service charges by the quantity of data retrieved. In contrast, most countries in South America still rely heavily on dial-up PC access and telephone charges are high for each minute of use. Regulations differ greatly; some countries like China have restrictions that favor national providers. National and regional portals have mounted a powerful challenge but it has not so far been possible to establish a single dominant global portal.[3]

- **E-zines** have created a veritable culture. There are literally thousands of e-zines (a recent list shows 3,500 titles), ranging from full-feature magazines like *Salon* and *Slate* to the Web sites of print publications like the *New York Times* and FT.com, and to specialized newsletters devoted to particular topics or regions. Anyone who has the interest and a little money can be an author and seek out an audience. But, as is typical of such ventures, many live on the edge financially.

  Even the true magazines have had financial difficulties. Slate.com experimented with a subscription charge and *Salon.com,* which is on the brink of bankrupty, offers a fee-based premium service.

  Advertising revenues have not been sufficient, and their growth has been disappointing.

- **E-music** and **e-videos** have seen substantial turmoil. The potential for distributing these materials without recompensing the copyright holders has enraged the record companies (see the discussion of Napster in Case 9.1). While there may be ways to limit free distribution, it remains difficult to distribute information-intensive materials, especially videos, over the "pipes" of the Internet. Because it takes a very long time to download a movie, movies ordered on the Internet are distributed in the old-fashioned way, on a DVD via Fed Ex.

- **E-books** would appear to have great potential, but slow electronic transmission and the consumer's reluctance to read on an electronic tablet stand in the way. Experiments with electronic books have not been successful. On the other hand, the day may come when books are no longer stocked on shelves or shipped but are printed on demand in a bookstore or at home. This possibility would drastically change the role of libraries. Instead of being stored on a shelf, books might be kept on CDs or in computer memory. A central electronic

---

[3]Robles, 2000, op. cit., no. 1.

library might meet most research needs. Users would have a choice of reading on a screen or printing out the information.

- **E-photo** processing has taken advantage of the rapid progress in digital photography, fast communication, and inexpensive storage. Initially it was just a matter of sending your film for processing and getting the pictures back on a diskette as well as in hardcopy. The field has changed with surprising speed. Digital is rapidly replacing film—it is estimated that by the end of 2003 there will be 16 million digital camera users taking 400 million digital pictures. Today, digital pictures are being uploaded to the central computer storage—Ofoto or Eframes, for example. There they can be viewed, edited, framed, and printed. The future may bring further changes as cheaper home printers or distributed printing at your local photo shop or drug store change the pattern once again (Case 9.3).

- **Health care** offers great e-business network opportunities. Medical information, practice management, and computerized billing and claims reimbursement systems have grown rapidly. WebMD is a leading source of medical information to the medical profession as well as consumers. It also offers WebMD Envoy, a provider of EDI services to physicians and others for claims processing, patient billing, and provider reimbursement. It may also be used for prescribing and ordering drugs and reporting the results of lab tests. WebMD Medical Manager handles physician practice management, including appointment scheduling, billing, and maintaining medical histories.

  On the other hand, fully integrated network applications that supply patient information to various providers are not yet widely used. It should be possible to retrieve health records, appointments, patient histories, and data on diagnoses and treatments for each patient from one central source. Network-based systems containing patient records widely accessible to health care providers are still largely to come. This reflects differences in the standards of hospital computer systems, problems with the protection of patient privacy, and high costs. The privacy of health care information has recently been a matter of controversy. One issue is whether explicit patient consent should be required before data about individual patients can be used for direct advertising purposes.

- **Government** is another potentially important source of large-scale efficiency gains. Computers are used by many government agencies to handle specialized records for many purposes—drivers' license and violation records, for example. A beginning is being made with electronic income tax returns, but generally government records are not yet widely accessible over public networks and there are thought to be security risks. There are many more possibilities to be exploited: collection of other taxes, licenses, government services and information, and even electronic voting.

E-government has become a new enthusiasm in many countries. Pollsters report that e-government is a big success in Singapore, but it may pose more difficult challenges in other countries. In one large developing country, local researchers suggested that e-government services would be difficult to establish in a region where a majority of people had never heard of the Internet and where few have computer connections. The researchers were encouraged to close down their activities because the results would conflict with government policy.[4]

- **E-learning.** "Although enthusiasts still argue that E-learning will eventually be huge—market estimates are in the multibillion dollar range—for now it has a decidedly mixed report card—there's a new caution in the air. Practicality and profits matter. Call it back-to-basics education."[5]

Education appears to offer a wide-open prospect for e-learning, one that transcends geographic boundaries. Some people have proposed on-line courses worldwide, to make learning available in poor countries at minimal cost, but it is turning out to be difficult to turn e-learning promise into practical applications. Still, many universities have begun on-line degree programs (MBAs, for example), relying entirely or almost entirely on virtual interaction between the instructor and student. The *U.S. News E-Learning Report* lists more than 1,000 programs. While some traditional distance-learning schools like the profit-making University of Phoenix and the University of Maryland claim some success, traditional bricks-and-ivy universities have recently been cutting back their efforts because of high costs and insufficient enrollments.

There have been numerous difficulties. E-learning calls for new types of teaching programs because learning over the Internet is simply different from classroom instruction. Labor costs are high because there is need for individual human interaction to manage chat-rooms and reply to questions. Finally, many universities have not been able to locate a sufficiently large market of prospective e-learning students.

---

[4]Correspondence with a former student engaged in this research.
[5]"Special Report: E-Learning." *U.S. News and World Report,* October 15, 2001; <*http://www.usnews.com/usnews/edu/elearning/articles/biz.htm*>.

The future of e-learning seems to lie in a different direction: corporate training programs. Companies paring back their training budgets hope to increase efficiency by turning to Internet-based training programs. A great deal depends on the nature of the instruction needed. Informational or "how to" learning such as specifications of a new product line or how to set up a new model of computer are suited to Web-based instruction.

On the other hand, personal interactions, especially networking with other company employees, are obviously less effective at a distance than at an old-fashioned training session. True, high-tech companies like Oracle and IBM are meeting a large part of their training needs through Web-based instruction, but it is not clear how quickly traditional companies are turning to e-learning, though some firms with large numbers of employees or franchisees (McDonald's) are doing so expeditiously.

Case 9.1
Napster and the Record Companies

The story of Napster is an interesting illustration of the potentials and risks of new dot-com ventures. Napster was the pioneer peer-to-peer music site, designed by a young Northeastern college student, Shawn Fanning, whose nickname was Napster. The idea was that people could download music from someone else's computer to their computers. This type of service, known as peer-to-peer file sharing, allows users to trade music encoded in the MP3 format, which compresses recordings into small and portable files without sacrificing quality.

Napster operated as an intermediary, providing lists of recordings available and making the connections from source to the destination. If someone requested a particular recording, Napster would search for it on members' open computers, copy it into a central server, and then transmit it to the individual making the request. No provision was made to compensate the copyright owner.

Napster quickly became popular among young people—by 2000 as many as 30 million people had downloaded the software and were trading recordings. Napster was called a social phenomenon because millions of individuals were willing to open their computers to the world. An incidental result was tremendous consumption of transmission capacity. Some university computer networks were greatly overloaded, sometimes clogged, because so many freshmen and sophomores were downloading each other's music. Moreover:

"Just as Napster wasn't a technological breakthrough, it also wasn't a bright business idea. It would have had tremendous difficulties turning a profit, because it was born as an innovation by eager college students and moneymaking wasn't initially a goal. In fact, the belated attempt to monetize its popularity forced Napster to become a corporation, thus making it an easy target for the music companies."[6]

The major record firms, appalled at the potential loss of revenue from copyrighted materials, sued Napster to block the freeloaders, claiming that the company encouraged illegal copying and distribution of copyrighted music on a massive scale. The court ordered Napster to bar copyrighted music from its web site, a move that shut down the service and unplugged its many users. After failure of an acquisition attempt by the huge European publishing firm Bertelsmann, Napster was finally closed.

But it is hard to keep such free service down; Napster clones like KazaA are providing similar services. The peer-to-peer services for music and video that are still available use systems that, unlike Napster, do not route the copied material through a central server. It is unlikely, however, that the courts will long permit continued illegal copying of copyrighted material by this alternative route.

A different approach was taken by the major record companies, which have established Rhapsody, a subscription service on Listen.com. For a monthly fee, subscribers can download current popular songs as well as material from the labels' archive libraries, but they can keep very little material in their computer memory or on CDs. Thus, the new services will protect copyright owners from illegal copying. More recently AOL has been experimenting with a service allowing subscribers to download music from a limited menu for 99 cents per recording. It is not yet clear whether such services will be popular.

Case 9.2
E-Bulletin Boards

Monster.com, the largest employment bulletin board on the Internet, has more than 20 million registered users. On a typical afternoon, many millions of job seekers are on line. Jobs are listed by geographic area and by function. In many cases it is possible to apply for the job on line.

---

[6]*<http://Knowledge.Wharton.upenn.edu/articles.cfm?articleid=14&articleid=222>.*

Economists have argued that Internet services like Monster.com will improve the operation of labor markets. They may make wages more uniform as prospective employees search out the best-paying jobs. They may also provide opportunities for "star" workers, outstanding salespeople, for example, to find suitable opportunities to make the best use of their talents and get the highest pay.

Paradoxically, computerized listings like Monster.com also demonstrate the shortcomings of e-based relationships: In the end, most human resources managers would not hire anybody without getting to know them in a personal interview.

Electronic real estate listings are also extremely useful, but, again, buyers usually prefer to look at a property before buying it. The same may be true of e-want ads, particularly the widely available personal ads.

Case 9.3
Eframes.com

Eframes is a good example of the evolution of entrepreneurial effort in an e-business. Started by 31-year-old Brian Dunham in 1999, Eframes has become a successful photo printing and framing company.

Dunham realized that computer storage was becoming cheaper. His idea was to persuade digital camera fans to put their pictures on the Eframes web site, free of charge, but to garner profits by selling printing services, framing, holiday cards, printed mugs, and T-shirts. Dunham points out that the photo printing market is extremely competitive (Kodak-owned Ofoto is a competitor), but profit margins on enlargements and printed products are high. The company has been growing rapidly—but in true e-business fashion, it has already been sold at least twice, once to a large firm that went bankrupt and once again to a digital photo enlarging and processing company.

There are some interesting questions about the future of this business. Not only has digital photography grown rapidly, its expansion is expected to continue for some years. But consumers have not moved nearly as rapidly to Internet processing as might have been expected. When film is processed, all the pictures on the roll are printed. In digital, the consumer may choose to print only the best pictures, or even just keep them on the computer instead of in a photo album. Moreover, unless a broadband connection is available, uploading to the processor's Web site can be troublesome. Camera fans usually want their prints quickly, more quickly than is possible with mail delivery.

One solution would be distributed processing, where pictures are uploaded to the Web and then picked up at a nearby camera store or drugstore. Technically, this is quite feasible. The problem is that network-printing facilities are costly and stores already have large investments in conventional processing machinery. Dunham suggests that after the store, the paper maker, and the machinery provider get their share, the margin for the on-line photo company would be razor-thin. An alternative approach is to drop off the camera's memory card at the store for processing. Finally, the costs of small printers that permit processing at home have been coming down rapidly. These are the kinds of trends that can challenge any e-business entrepreneur.

Chapter 10
The E-Business Experience

"When the tulip mania dies down, all that remains are pretty flowers. When bubbles burst, nothing is left but soapy residue. But, the Internet revolution, for all its speculative excesses, really is changing the world."[1]

It has been interesting to see the broad range of commercial possibilities opened by the network revolution. Venture capitalists have underwritten many "blue sky" ideas. Some of them have worked out brilliantly, but, as the dot-com crash demonstrates, others have failed dismally. What seems to give the best chance for success?

E-BUSINESS INNOVATION: SUSTAINING OR DISRUPTIVE?

New ideas are not commercially relevant until they have been marketed successfully as useful innovations. Because this is a challenging task that calls for significant experience and market position, most business innovation is incremental. Improved products are usually modifications of existing goods and services introduced by established vendors. It is relatively easy for these firms to sound out what their customers want and adapt products to meet these needs.

Yet a remarkable aspect of IT and e-business innovation has been that it has often come as an abrupt change introduced by newcomers. Many e-business innovations have been entirely new products and services for which there was not yet a market or which represented a new way of meeting existing needs. Some new IT and e-business products have been brought to market by new firms that displaced established enterprises. On occasion this has hap-

---

[1]Adam Cohen. "Editorial Observer: PayPal and Other Post-Bubble Signs of Life on the Internet." *New York Times*, February 7, 2002.

pened even when the established firms were the original inventors of the concept—Apple Computer's "desk top," now shared by Microsoft Windows, originated in Xerox's Palo Alto Research Center (PARC) but Xerox never succeeded in promoting it commercially.

The distinction between sustaining and disruptive innovations helps to explain this phenomenon. Sustaining innovation meets the evolving needs of existing customers. It represents gradual adjustment to requirements of customers in the firm's current markets. Disruptive innovation represents a new approach, meeting different needs with new technology, often in altogether new markets. In the words of Robert Reich: "So-called 'killer apps'—fundamentally new ideas, products, and ways of doing business—alter the terms of competition for entire industries."[2]

Drawing an analogy with the theory of scientific revolutions that some innovations represent paradigm shifts and replace standard science, Harvard's Clayton Christensen[3] argues that, in the face of disruptive innovations, great companies with apparently strong products may not keep up: They are good at sustaining innovations but cannot achieve disruptive developments. They do not make it precisely because "they do it right"—when they gradually improve their products for existing customers, industry leaders may not sufficiently take into account the threat of radical innovations. Again and again, digital electronic equipment—disk drives, memories, servers, etc.—and its e-business applications have demonstrated these kinds of radical changes.

What does this mean in the e-business world? On the one hand, there are sometimes opportunities to bring radical new kinds of business to market that compete even with large established enterprises. Certainly, this has happened often in the IT/e-business revolution. On the other hand, only a minuscule fraction of the radical innovators successfully commercialize their disruptive innovations; many failed dot-com services faded away as quickly as they appeared, as I am reminded by the Obongo bar that still graces my computer screen long after the service has ceased.

It is a tough challenge for newcomers to make their way into established markets. They must be able to build market recognition quickly, to rapidly create enough volume to gain economies of scale perhaps at little or no profit. But the innovator must not lose sight of the continued need for cash (earned or borrowed) and of what the long run viability of the new business demands.

Moreover, once an e-business has been established, it must constantly be tweaked—by sustaining innovation. It must continue to adapt to customer needs and to take advantage of the latest technology, without getting too far

---

[2]Robert B. Reich (2002). *The Future of Success.* New York: Random House, Vintage Books, p. 18.
[3]Clayton M. Christensen (1997). *The Innovator's Dilemma.* New York: HarperCollins.

ahead of its customers' competencies. Some e-business firms have done all this successfully on their own. Others have been acquired by established firms. Plenty of others did not make it.

The scenario for disruptive innovations tends to look like this:

- Disruptive technologies or e-business projects are developed, sometimes but not always within established firms.
- Marketing personnel seek reactions from current customers, who may not want radical changes.
- Established firms step up the pace of sustaining technological development in an effort to meet customer needs without disruption.
- New companies enter the market and succeed in marketing disruptive technologies because:
  –The innovation costs significantly less.
  –The innovation offers a significantly more advanced product.
  –The innovation represents a significant improvement in quality of service or even a new service.
- The new entrant gains significant market share.
- Established firms belatedly jump on the bandwagon to defend their markets, perhaps by introducing comparable innovations or by acquiring the innovator.

Some familiar examples of what can happen with innovation are:

- Successful.
  –Dell uses its strategy of producing custom PCs to become the dominant seller.
  –eBay continues to expand, ultimately acquiring PayPal.
  –Amazon expands from books into other products.
- Acquisition.
  –IBM acquires Lotus Development in order to market Lotus Notes.
  –AOL acquires Netscape.
- Failures.
  –Large telecoms—WorldCom, Adelphia, Pacific Crossing—go bankrupt.
  –Bankruptcy hits Web grocer Webvan, electronic payment broker Cybercash, retailer E-Toys, and many more.

MAKING ALTERNATIVE E-BUSINESS MODELS WORK

Much depends on the business model a company is working with. Possibilities are very different depending on whether the concern is transactions between businesses, within a business, or with consumers.

Intra- or inter-business e-operations seek to improve the efficiency of management, to reduce costs, and to accomplish tasks automatically rather than with human intervention. Because of competitive pressures, businesses are accustomed to seek low-cost, efficient solutions. Unfortunately, they are often tied to legacy systems operated by current employees who may be reluctant to make changes.

Ultimately, the decision whether to implement a new electronic system is an investment decision, based on expectations of net return—but efforts to convert to e-business systems are considerably more risky and complicated than conventional investments in physical capacity. Even if the new computerized system has had extensive application elsewhere, the contractor may find it difficult to reconcile it with a firm's existing systems, with hardware and software currently available, and with the specific needs of the firm's suppliers or customers. Promised gains in efficiency and cost reductions may not materialize.

The more innovative the solution, the greater the risk. Firms with large established operations will hesitate to take advantage of new e-business solutions. It is not surprising, then, that many banks have been reluctant to switch to Internet banking systems. Newer operations that are not heavily invested in existing systems or are not yet established in the market may find an e-business strategy more attractive.

E-business systems directed toward the consumer have somewhat different objectives, and quite different problems. E-retailing firms seek to extend their markets through another sales channel, the Internet. In cases like travel services, tickets, and stock brokerage that offer distinctly improved, faster service without human intervention, how the Web site interacts with the purchaser is critical. The computer screen must invite the consumer to participate. It must be intuitively easy to operate. It must provide quick responses. Many e-business firms directed at consumers have discovered that consumers will often click on their site and window-shop but fail to carry through the transaction because it seems complicated.

The consumer e-business plan must also deal with fulfillment. Though some products can be transmitted directly over the Internet, doing so may require greater transmission capacity and technical knowledge than is available to the typical consumer. For example, the majority of people who purchase computer programs over the Internet ask for delivery on CDs rather than electronically even though delivery by mail or express poses additional costs.

Information services like portals, search engines, and classified advertising face altogether different issues. In these cases, the challenge is to find a reliable, growing source of revenue. Perhaps consumers can be persuaded to pay for subscriptions, but so long as such services are available free, the market will remain limited. Perhaps advertising will increase—or at least that is what most service providers are hoping.

PRIVACY AND SECURITY ON THE INTERNET

"Advances in computer technology have made it possible for detailed information about people to be compiled and shared more easily and cheaply than ever. That's good for society as a whole and for individual consumers. At the same time, as personal information becomes more accessible, each of us—companies, associations, government agencies, and consumers—must take precautions to protect against the misuse of that information."[4]

Questions of privacy and security have become a major concern in connection with B2C e-business and e-mail. Over 90 percent of web sites collect some personal identifying information. About half collect demographic references (e.g., gender, preferences, zip code).[5] The use of personal information, including credit card numbers, e-mail addresses, and personal addresses, is unavoidable in many e-business transactions. The issue is the confidentiality of these data. Can it be misused?

There are significant differences between use of personal information by the vendor who originally received the information, by secondary vendors to whom it has been sold, and by illegal users. For the initial vendor, demographic and personal information may be enormously useful in analyzing market trends: Who are the buyers and how may advertising and product specifications be better adapted to their needs? Such data may also be used to improve customer service, for example, to suggest to book purchasers related titles they may want to consider. It may also be helpful in targeting advertising and e-mail to former customers.

Many firms assure their clients that data will go into secure sites and that proprietary information will not be passed on to other users. Many do not. Much private information is sold to other firms that use it, for example, as the basis for advertising messages.

---

[4]Federal Trade Commission, October 4, 2001; <*http://www.ftc.gov/privacy/index.html*>.
[5]"Georgetown Internet Privacy Policy Survey: Report to the Federal Trade Commission, 1999. Study director Mary J. Culnan; <*http://www.msb.edu/faculty/culnan/gipps/mmrpt.pdf*>.

Finally, there are unsolicited uses, such as advertising (spam) or illegal uses like unapproved purchases using a customer's credit card number. Hackers may use e-mail addresses and related information to enter a computer memory, retrieve confidential data, or otherwise damage the computer files. It is therefore not surprising that some prospective buyers are reluctant to enter confidential information into the Internet.

Laws have been passed to protect confidentiality. In implementing the provisions of the Gramm-Leach-Bliley Act of 1999 that govern the privacy of consumers' financial information, the FTC rule limits disclosure by financial institutions of "nonpublic personal information." Companies must post their privacy policy. Consumers must be given the opportunity to opt out, allowing them to withhold private information.

In the United States, people are accustomed to giving out their credit card numbers, but even so some observers feel that the risk to privacy is a significant drag on Web purchases. In other countries, it appears that consumers may be more concerned about releasing credit card numbers and similar private information than in the United States. This reluctance may well present a barrier to e-commerce.

Cyber-security is a related but more serious issue. Conceptually, it is possible for foreign governments or terrorists to enter a nation's computers through the Internet. Secret information could be acquired. Data and communication could be interfered with and computer viruses spread. Security is a challenge; the goal is to maintain maximum network interconnection at minimum security risk.

Case 10.1
E-Mail and Spam

"In a popularity contest, 'bulk e-mailers' would rank just above child pornographers."[6] Spam—unsolicited commercial messages directed to your e-mail account—have become the scourge of the Internet. Users are finding their e-mail accounts cluttered by numerous useless messages. Some of these commercials come from firms with which they have done business; others are sent by commercial spammers, who often send dubious propositions with misleading subject lines (computer viruses are often spread this way). Internet service providers like AOL are overwhelmed with this excess traffic. Hundreds of millions of such messages are being sent every day. It is estimated that they make up 30 to 40 percent of e-mail activity.

E-mail account users often delete these messages without reading them but that, too, takes time and can be a nuisance. For the senders,

---

[6]Brad Stone and Jennifer Lin. "Spanning the World." *Newsweek,* August 19, 2002.

the response rate is very low, perhaps only 25 returns from a million messages, but because the cost of sending the messages is also minimal, advertising by spamming remains a profitable business.

Spam operations are often fly-by-night businesses. They obtain e-mail addresses by using commercial software to scour the Web for addresses on bulletin boards and directories. Sometimes they simply send to common names on mail servers, hoping to find a match, or they randomly generate addresses.

U.S. ISPs and company networks have policies against spam and programs designed to intercept it before it reaches individual accounts; to avoid the barriers, spam messages are often sent through computers in the Far East, where their origin is difficult to trace, and subject lines are usually not informative or contain numbers. The worldwide connectivity that is the Internet is precisely the reason why spam is difficult to control. If it is blocked from one location, there is always another place from which to send it.

The volume of e-mail communication has been increasing by leaps and bounds. This is turning out to be a serious cost—not transmission cost but time cost, because it takes so long to read and respond to it. Some firms report that their managers get as many as 100 e-mails a day and take as long as four hours to deal with them. Tempting though it is, it is not wise to simply erase the whole lot; it is hard to gauge the importance of a message just from the content line.

Computer programs are being written that rate incoming e-mails according to their importance. The user specifies parameters to guide the evaluation. These parameters may also adjust automatically to the user's recent e-mail deletion practice. This is a case where one form of technical progress, e-mail, calls for a new remedy.

WHAT WORKS AND WHAT DOESN'T

Here some thoughts on what works in e-business and what doesn't.

The most successful and lasting ventures seem to have at least one of the following characteristics:

- There is considerable cost reduction to users, as in financial transactions like securities trading (e*Trade).
- There are significant improvements in convenience and range of selection (Amazon).
- Fulfillment is relatively simple (electronic) or can be linked to an existing business (grocery deliveries from existing supermarkets).

- Savings on management and clerical labor are substantial, enough to fully offset the costs of hardware, programming, and transition to a new system.
- The electronic programs are easy to access and use (e-tickets).
- The products being traded are standardized and can be readily described on the Web.
- Time is important (e-mail).

What seems *not* to work? The least successful ventures, those that have had the shortest lives, appear to have the following characteristics:

- To succeed, they must reach a large proportion of the relevant market. It is not wise to assume that all consumers want to switch to buying on the Web. The Web marketplace is growing but it is likely to remain limited for some time. Many people go to the mall not just to try on clothes and shop but also to socialize—surfing on a computer is a very solitary activity.
- Fulfillment is expensive. Poor and costly fulfillment has been one of the big problems with e-groceries. Amazon has also found fulfillment a tremendous challenge and has passed some of its delivery tasks on to brick-and-mortar book sellers.
- The products are diverse and customized. Because custom parts, for example, require extensive negotiation, even cooperative efforts, they are ill-suited for trade on an Internet exchange.
- The programming required to order is complex. This is still a big barrier. Many computer users start the ordering process and then abandon it because of its complexity or for fear that it is being transmitted incorrectly.
- Legacy equipment and programming still meet current needs even though they may not be as efficient as a Web-based system.
- The costs of hardware, software, and transition are uncertain.
- Sophisticated equipment is required, particularly fast broadband access to the Internet. Only a fraction of PCs are linked to the Web with high-speed broadband service that makes it easy to get colorful catalogs and to order. Broadband, based on cable, DSL, and satellite access, has taken longer to develop than some experts had hoped and it remains costly. As a result, only a fraction of users, perhaps no more than 10 percent, are in a position to take advantage of sophisticated broadband applications.
- Prospects for making revenues are unclear (portals and e-zines).

Experience has provided much information on what works and what does not. The potential of new many Web-based operations is still very large. There are still promising types of Web-based operations that have not been exploited. Internet-based operations must, however, be closely integrated with the old sectors of the economy. It is also likely that in the future, fewer free services will be available on the Web; more services will charge subscriptions or fees.

Case 10.2
What Caused the Dot-com Crash?

As we know, the heady period of technical and e-business innovation that marked the 1990s boom did not last. The years since 2000 have been disastrous for many dot-com firms. The drastic drop of the stock market indexes from an early 2000 peak (Figure 1.2, page 13) does not tell the whole story, either for the soft dot-com firms that provide programming or e-business services or for the hard, capital-intensive companies building high-tech equipment or using it to provide the communications backbone.

Why did the industry go through such an abrupt feast and famine cycle? Does the crash mean that there are basic problems with the dot-com business model, that there is no future for e-business? Does it call for reorganization of the industry, for perhaps drastic change in its structure?

In many parts of the industry—hardware, communications, and e-business—the story is one of both unrealistic expectations *and* wild competition. "Irrational exuberance" certainly characterized the Internet stock market boom of the 1990s. While broader stock price indexes were high—higher, indeed, than traditional price-earnings ratios would support—prices of the leading Internet-related stocks were truly astronomical. But the story of this period is not simply one of stock market manipulation or accounting irregularities.

To begin with, the entrepreneurial culture of Silicon Valley was the source of an explosion of business building. The young people who started Internet-related businesses were not initially out to make huge profits. Like the young Bill Gates, many started in an upstairs bedroom. They had little knowledge of business management. Most important, they did not have clear expectations about how or when they might make profits. They sought financial support from family members and from venture capital firms. They were highly competitive. But while many started on the same path, only a minority survived.

Venture capital has played an important role not only for financing but also as an incubator for many new firms. The venture capitalist provides guidance on business strategy, sometimes provides working space, and finds experienced businesspeople to manage the proposed dot-com enterprise. Dot-com business managers have often been a generation older than the firms' founders.

Once a new dot-com firm was operating and there was a glimmer of a prospect of making profits, "going public" was the next step. The enormous gains made from an initial public offering (IPO) turned many a young entrepreneur into a millionaire, even a billionaire. In a heated, excessively optimistic atmosphere, the upsurge of stock prices turned out to be a self-fulfilling prophecy. Kindleberger, writing about past *Manias, Panics, and Crashes,* says, "What happens basically is that some event changes the economic outlook. New opportunities for profits are seized, and overdone, in ways so closely resembling irrationality as to constitute a mania."[7]

In the dot-com case, the new developments were communication links, computer programs, and e-business possibilities. The rise in stock prices built expectations of further gains, which would in many cases end up validating the original unrealistic expectations. Highly valued stocks were turned into "currency" that could be used to purchase other ventures. This enabled many entrepreneurs to sell out their overvalued stock at extraordinary prices. It encouraged mergers and acquisitions that supposedly provided gains from scale as well as immediate financial benefits.

Of course, the process also worked in the downward direction when it began to be recognized that the prospects for profits were poor. Many e-entrepreneurs have found it difficult to make a profit— sometimes even to get income—from their sites. Web advertising, like banners on top of Web pages, has not paid off well. Few people are willing to pay for Web-based subscriptions. Few e-firms have been able to achieve profitable scale. Fast modem connections (broadband) are not yet widespread enough for applications like video. High fulfillment costs eat into the revenues of Web retailers.

At those times when business appeared to be expanding rapidly and expectations were high, venture capitalists closed their eyes to such difficulties. In the 1990s, even firms with deficient financial performance were able to float IPOs at wildly inflated prices. Stocks whose prices had increased far beyond what could be justified by their probable return were used to make acquisitions.

But as growth slowed and confidence faltered, venture capital and IPO money dried up. The crash was unexpectedly rapid. Squeezed by

---

[7]Charles P. Kindleberger (1996). *Manias, Panics, and Crashes: A History of Financial Crises,* 3rd ed. New York: Wiley, p. 2.

lack of liquid cash, many Web sites closed down and others are on the brink of failure. Some have started subscription services in an effort to get cash flow. Some have been selling out to larger scale brick-and-mortar businesses.

The shakeout has been under way since mid-2000. In December 2001, *Fortune* magazine reported that 384 dot-coms had "passed on" in 2001. The "In Memoriam" list ranges from Acusa.com to Zydeco.com.[8]

Related but somewhat different problems hit the hardware providers, especially the telecoms, in 2002. *The Economist* front-paged its story as "The Great Telecoms Crash."[9] The telecom sector showed enormous promise as a result of regulatory reform and technical progress. Regulations passed in 1996 opened local telecom markets to unregulated competition. At the same time, demand for communications was burgeoning with the growth of cellular phone communications and the Internet. In particular, requirements for fiberoptic channels were expected to grow rapidly to meet expected demand for video communication.

The result was a tremendous effort to build nationwide fiberoptic networks, but by 2001 it was apparent that there was a vast excess of capacity. Demand simply had not grown as fast as anticipated. Too many competitors had invested in network capacity. And, paradoxically, new technology had made it possible to accommodate many more messages simultaneously on one fiberoptic cable than had earlier been anticipated. Capacity utilization in the Internet fiberoptic system was said to be as low as 3 percent.

To complicate matters, most of the construction had been financed by borrowing and the heavily leveraged ventures were soon running out of cash. Efforts to meet profit targets by using accounting tricks (in some cases like WorldCom by outright fraud) eroded investor and creditor confidence. As a result, major new telecom and cable TV ventures—WorldCom, Adelphia, and Qwest Communications—failed.

Under the title "New Economy, Old Economy: A Shakeout Is a Shakeout" *Knowledge@Wharton* reported that George Day, a Wharton marketing professor who has studied old economy shakeouts from the invention of the railroad to the advent of the personal computer, found that this new economy shakeout is not much different from the old: "Far too many players come in, there's lots of excitement, high visibility, low barriers to entry. . . . It is like every other shakeout, just a lot

[8]E. Florian. "Dead and (Mostly) Gone Dot-coms." *Fortune,* December 24, 2001.
[9]"New Economy, Old Economy: A Shakeout is a Shakeout." *Knowledge@Wharton,* July 26, 2002; *<http://knowledge.wharton.upenn.edu/articles.cfm?catid=4&articleid=318>*.

faster magnified by free-flowing capital, incubators, and the tendency for everyone to converge in the same business model."[10]

Some e-firms have grown rapidly and continue to do well—in e-retail, auctions, and brokerage, for example. Longer-run prospects in some other fields remain bright even though e-firms there may be in deep trouble currently.

We have come to the realization that e-business will not simply replace conventional business. In some operations, like brokerage, e-business is highly advantageous. In others, it offers niche markets or expands the number of outlets to existing businesses, as it does in book selling. In still others, e-business produces entirely new products like portals and e-zines where the key to profit is still elusive. Still others, like video, are blocked for now by technical barriers that must still be overcome.

It is too early to write off IT/e-business. While the bubble has burst, the underlying technological progress remains. Much of the new hardware, software, and knowledge is still relevant and useful. Indeed, its use is growing. We cannot yet predict the variety of new applications that will appear as technology and management better match the market.

Concluding Comment (Part II)

- Lots of diverse possibilities have been opened by the electronic network. What factors seem to contribute to success of e-business ventures?
  - –Big savings to consumers.
  - –Improved convenience and range of services.
  - –Ease of fulfillment and linkage to existing business operations;
  - –Savings in personnel costs.
  - –Ease of use.

- What does not work?
  - –Assumption that all purchasers want to migrate to the Web.
  - –Poorly organized and costly fulfillment.
  - –Complex programming or selection processes.
  - –Need for high speed broadband connections.

---

[10]"New Economy, Old Economy: A Shakeout is a Shakeout." *Knowledge@Wharton,* July 26, 2002; <*http://knowledge.wharton.upenn.edu/articles.cfm?catid=4&articleid=318*>.

Part III
The Economics of E-Business

Chapter 11

The Economics of the Knowledge Economy and E-Business

As with other industrial revolutions, important technical changes lie behind the development of IT and e-business. Scientific progress and high-tech investments are critical underpinnings of the changes taking place. Once the physical backbone and other organs of the network have been set up, what is revolutionary is the overwhelming reliance of the new economy on information and knowledge. E-business is not so much about equipment as about programs, data files, and transmission of information; knowledge is therefore the critical ingredient. The new economy is made possible by the accumulation of knowledge.

KNOWLEDGE CAPITAL AND HARDWARE CAPITAL

In some ways, the accumulation of knowledge is like the accumulation of physical capital, but in others, knowledge capital accumulates very differently. This has important implications for evaluating the prospects for a knowledge-based economy.

Many economists remind us that building a stock of knowledge requires saving and investment just as physical capital does. The clearest example is the accumulation of human capital, the economist's term for an increase in a society's level of educational attainment. Education calls for the use of resources for building schools and hiring teachers. Moreover, education means that students must forego the income they could have earned by unskilled employment to sit in the classroom and learn, hopefully so that they will make up these lost earnings by the higher income they will make later once they are in skilled or professional jobs. Job-specific training, apprenticeships, and learning on the job also call for using resources now as an investment in future returns.

Research and development (R&D) similarly is an explicit process of allocating work effort and equipment to build knowledge, in the expectation that there will be a future payoff. (Note that basic research, where the reward may be uncertain and far in the future, is likely to be supported by public funds, whereas applied research, which will yield a return with greater certainty and more quickly, is often supported directly by business.)

Knowledge capital has some characteristics that make it very different from physical capital, primary among them permanence, fungibility, and economies of scale. What do these characteristics mean?

- *Knowledge capital is permanent.* Once a discovery has been made, it will not be unmade. Unlike physical capital, knowledge capital does not depreciate with age or use. Admittedly, as new ideas are advanced, they may reduce the usefulness of old ones, so technical progress does involve "creative destruction." But knowledge does not disappear or depreciate. There may be a recession, with reduced investment and possibly even a deterioration in physical capital stock, but knowledge once known is always there to be applied. The technical expertise and the science underlying the IT and e-business revolution remain to be used as needed in the future.

- *Knowledge is fungible.* This is the *externality* feature of knowledge: The stock of technical information developed by one firm or in one country may be used anywhere. True, patents, copyrights, and trade secrets help a firm to take advantage of new inventions. In the short run, some information is distributed through licensing (or in some countries through piracy). But ultimately knowledge cannot be kept hidden; it becomes widely available for use. Potential applications of knowledge can and do transcend firm and national boundaries.

- *Knowledge offers economies of scale.* The striking thing about knowledge in contrast to physical capital is that its use by one firm does not prevent its use by others. Little or no additional cost is incurred if additional users take advantage of the same invention—effectively, the economies of scale are without limit. The more users of a new idea, the better off society is!

- *Production of knowledge and its use are interactive.* By this we mean that new ideas are seldom created or applied in isolation; they result from the interactions of researchers at universities and businesspeople working together. It is not surprising, then, that many new developments arise in geographic clusters—that IT/e-business operations are so heavily clustered in Silicon Valley, for example.

- *Knowledge has always been important, but it has never been as important as it is in today's economy.* The new economy is a knowledge economy, the result of intellectual creativity. Its operation puts a premium on skills, some relatively mundane, like data entry, others highly complex, like advanced programming. It is not surprising, then, that the new economy originated in advanced countries where levels of education and technical expertise are high.

Information technology is a somewhat special type of knowledge. It is best described as *general purpose knowledge* in that many IT advances can be used in a wide range of products and procedures. The same line of chip technology can power computers, cell phones, and automobile controls, for example. The same basic programming enters into numerous different applications.

The contribution of general purpose technologies is likely to be much broader and larger than technology embodied in specific machinery. According to Brynjolfsson and Hitt, general technologies "are beneficial mostly because they facilitate complementary innovations."[1] The idea here is that general technologies have broad applications. They can potentially alter the way business is organized and managed, affecting productivity by reducing the need for human interaction, enlarging the scope of control, and reducing geographic limitations.

As we have noted, knowledge spreads across the world, but knowledge economics is likely to be particularly advantageous to highly educated countries, even small ones like Israel or Finland. Significant barriers stand in the way of growth of the knowledge economy in the developing countries. With some critical exceptions, the accumulation and utilization of knowledge is usually sequential. You must learn to walk before you can run. Similarly, a certain level of technical and educational attainment is required before advanced computer software can be used effectively. The presence of advanced hardware may not be enough, which explains the concern of development economists with "appropriate" technology. The need to prepare for high technology with education may remain a challenge to the introduction of advanced knowledge-intensive innovations in many less developed countries.

ECONOMICS AND E-BUSINESS

Does the economics of e-business really represent a revolutionary change? What are the special characteristics of e-business? Or is it simply another way to do business, a variation from accustomed ways but not all that different? Does e-business really translate into a new economy?

Economists are still arguing about these questions, but it is clear that e-business does produce some significant changes that have a place in economic theory, among them:

- Low transaction and communication cost.

---

[1]Erik Brynjolfsson and Lorin M. Hitt (2000). "Beyond Computation: Information Technology, Organizational Transformation, and Business Performance. *Journal of Economic Perspectives,* 14 (4): 23-48; <*http://ebusiness.mit.edu/erik*>.

- Increased competition.
- Economies of scale.
- First-mover advantages.
- Externalities.
- Technical change offsetting diminishing returns.

Let's look at how these changes play out:

- An important aspect of e-business is a dramatic reduction in transaction and communication costs. The reduced cost of transactions may have profound implications for the way businesses are organized, as we note in more detail later.
- Network contacts offer the possibility of a vastly increased intensity and range of competition. On the basis of e-business contacts, firms can deal with a greatly increased number of potential suppliers and customers, locally and all over the world.
- The optimal scale of an e-business is very large, because once the computer programs and networks have been set up, marginal costs are very low. Each additional transaction costs practically nothing. This may mean that a firm operating at very large scale can overwhelm its smaller competitors. Much of the activity in e-business has been about gaining advantages of scale in order to acquire much more pricing power. Amazon's "get big quick" strategy is a good example. This has been a factor in the concentration of software/programming and e-commerce firms and in growing alliances between many of them.
- On the other hand, there may also be room for smaller specialized Web-based firms that occupy niche markets that were not feasible before the advent of e-business. The narrow focus of some of these firms enables them to achieve economies of scale, but within very specialized markets.
- There is great value in being a first mover—establishing a market position before others are even aware there is a market. Since it is often complex and costly to change programs, the first program to have an established user base may maintain an advantage even if more effective or more sophisticated programs try to enter the market. Setting the standard is the way to obtain, and often to maintain, a dominant position.
- In principle, it can be argued that e-business software and hardware must encounter diminishing returns as other inputs do. As more IT investments are made, their marginal contribution to output should fall. In practice, however, new IT investments often modify the entire production process, even the entire organization Interactions between

new investments and technical change produce gains beyond what might be expected if the interactions are ignored.

An example is the continuous stream of faster, more sophisticated chips. These have made possible the real-time video and audio processing abilities of modern PCs, something that was simply beyond the reach of computers using older, less advanced chips. Another example is broadband communication that has made possible high-speed information-intensive communications like teleconferencing and video on demand.

- Innovative e-business schemes or programs often have externalities, advantages that extend beyond the original developer. New products and methods rise on the shoulders[2] of existing programs, extending them in ways that the originator had not envisioned. These important externalities may not be captured by the original developer but they are of benefit to the economy.

COASE TRANSACTION COST AND E-BUSINESS

Nobel Prize-winning economist Ronald Coase argued[3] that transaction costs influence the organization of a company. Transaction costs include the physical effort of searching for low-price, high-quality suppliers and arranging supply contracts, orders, and payments. The costs are affected by the difficulty or ease of communication. They also include an important component of reliability and trust: Will the supplier provide the product on time and to specification? Will the bill be paid?

Does e-commerce make a difference in the transaction costs of purchasers and suppliers? E-commerce is in fact another step in the trend toward decline in the costs of obtaining supplies. It can greatly reduce the costs of carrying out transactions—selecting, ordering, payment—while at the same time greatly increasing the number of potential suppliers, because firms from all over the world can offer products. In some cases, e-markets broaden participation and the efficiency of competitive price determination.

Does e-commerce potentially change the structure of an industry from vertically integrated firms toward more outsourcing? Since e-commerce reduces transaction costs with outsiders, it seems likely to allow for more outsourcing.

Changing fashions in the organization of industries and service businesses illustrate the considerable impact of changes in communication and transaction costs. Hierarchical structures of management are being decentralized. Production of simple standardized products, once the key to modern mass production, is

---

[2]The reference is to the famous statement of physicist Isaac Newton (1642-1727): "If I have seen farther than others, it is because I have stood on the shoulders of giants."
[3]Ronald Coase (1937). "The Nature of the Firm." *Economica,* 4: 386-405.

being replaced by customized (made to order) or semi-custom production methods, which are made possible by computerized order and production systems.

Supplies and services that are costly to "transact out" are done in integrated firms, in house; things that can be easily and reliably purchased from outsiders are often obtained from specialized independent suppliers—outsourced. The days of the huge vertically integrated firm may be numbered. This is already apparent in the auto industry where parts suppliers at GM and Ford have been turned into independent firms. It is also reflected in business process outsourcing (BSO). An increasing number of firms are outsourcing basic business activities like payroll processing; handling of orders, deliveries, and complaints, operation of computer centers, and other specialized functions. There are even virtual factories where everything except the general management function is outsourced.

Many tasks can be handled electronically. Often, they are carried out efficiently at far greater scale and with greater technical expertise than is available in a small or medium-sized firm. We must remember, though, that questions of quality and reliability are not easily handled electronically. It may still be necessary to produce some essential components in-house.

In the opposite direction, transaction costs within the firm can also be greatly reduced as a result of Internet or intranet communication, though most often in large-scale, geographically dispersed companies. Just as the telegraph and the telephone were critical to the creation of giant corporations,[4] today e-mail and data communication lie behind the increasingly huge scale of national and international corporations.

Hal Varian, Dean of the School of Information Management and Systems at the University of California at Berkeley, summed it up like this: "You don't need a new economics to understand the 'new economy.' . . . What has changed are the transaction costs."[5] This means that there are forces in both directions, toward increased outsourcing and specialization and toward larger size and more integration.

We can be sure that there will be changes, but we cannot be sure what the outcome for the structure of any industry is ultimately going to be.

COMPETITION AND MONOPOLY

Is it really true that "better information will move markets closer to the textbook model of perfect competition"?[6] The statement may be an exaggeration. True, e-commerce has the potential for improving market performance, but the

---

[4]Alfred D. Chandler (1977). *The Visible Hand.* Cambridge, MA: Harvard University Press.
[5]Nal Varian. "Economic Scene: The Usual Decorous Waltz Between Prices and Sales Becomes a Lively Tango in the Wolrd of Online Sales." *New York Times,* December 19, 2002.
[6]Thomas S. Siems. "B2B E-Commerce: Why the Economy Lives." Federal Reserve Bank of Dallas, Southwest Economy, July/August 2000, p. 1.

economist's concept of perfect competition calls for identical products having many suppliers and purchasers and that is not a realistic assumption for e-business. On the contrary, e-business may make it easier to differentiate products to meet customer specifications.

Even if we recognize that competition is imperfect, e-commerce may increase the scope and intensity of competition as long as there is potential for market entry. Searching for the lowest price used to be costly; now it can be done automatically. Firms used to rely on a few nearby suppliers; now their supply sources can be far more dispersed.

The expanded scope of competition explains why Internet exchanges have been a way for firms to reduce the costs of supplies. The effort of finding low-cost suppliers is greatly reduced. Traditional supplier firms are forced by low-cost competitors to seek improved efficiency and lower costs.

PRODUCT DIFFERENTIATION

The electronic IT world is a classic example of Schumpeter's idea of creative destruction. Schumpeterian economics[7] is at the opposite extreme from the classical economist's concept of perfect competition. In place of many competing buyers and sellers of identical products, Schumpeter visualized a world in which producers try to differentiate their products, each seeking to establish a protected quasi-monopolistic market position.

There has been much debate among economists about whether the costs of product differentiation—particularly branding and advertising—offset the advantages. Today's consensus is that they do. Product differentiation is a central ingredient of economic progress. It provides incentives for firms to add new features, improve quality, and introduce new technology. As new and better technologies appear, they displace the old systems. That's what we mean by *creative destruction*. The crowding-out of traditional methods by new ones improves the productive power of the economy.

This process has been seen repeatedly in the IT world. It forces even the leading producers to adopt updated versions of their products lest a newcomer beat them competitively, as has happened on many occasions. The hot competition between chip producers Intel and Advanced Micro Devices (AMD) is an example.

INNOVATION

While technological change is extremely rapid in microelectronic hardware and software, large firms have often failed to exploit the newest technologies. Economists speak of an innovations dilemma:

---

[7]Joseph A. Schumpeter (, 1942, 1975). *Capitalism, Socialism, and Democracy.* New York: Harper.

*"Companies that are responsive to their customers actually risk get-
ting locked into a set of arrangements that precludes them from
grasping the competitive advantages of innovation. . . . Large established firms are not very good at fully developing and commercializ-
ing technologies that disrupt their existing markets and procedures.
The more effectively a company is tied into its network of customers
and suppliers, the more likely it is to sustain a course of innovation
and maintain its present position within existing markets and technology. The less likely it will be to undertake radical innovation."*[8]

This is the case of sustaining innovation as contrasted to disruptive innovation that we have already talked about.

ECONOMIES OF SCALE

The introduction of computerized systems potentially increases competition.
Competition is strengthened when the range of competitors increases—more firms,
some from very far away, can compete for the same business. But IT systems may
also reduce competition; in some cases, they may even encourage monopoly.

In knowledge-based network products, there is tremendous payoff for
increased scale. Initial costs may sometimes be high, but the additional cost of
selling more product (the marginal cost) is very low. Once a product has been
developed, a sophisticated program, for example, selling it into a larger market may call for little more than stamping additional CDs and printing pretty
cardboard boxes. For network operations, Metcalfe's law produces enormous
gains simply from the interconnectivity of millions of potential users.

The economies of scale are an enormous incentive to expansion and,
where possible, sector domination. At the same time, they facilitate the process
of market concentration, because the smaller competitor inevitably incurs
higher unit costs and often lower unit revenues than the larger firm. Economies
of scale often lead to dominant firms with monopoly or close to monopoly
market shares. The situation of Microsoft in operating systems and in office
program suites is a good illustration (Case 11.1).

Sometimes scale advantages lead to the "survival of the biggest" rather
than of the fittest.

FIRST-MOVER ADVANTAGE

The first mover is simply the first firm to enter a new market. The firm may be
offering an altogether new product or service or may be carving out a new seg-

---

[8]BRIE-IGCC E-conomy Project (2001). *Tracking a Transformation: E-Commerce and the
Terms of Competition in Industries.* Washington: Brookings Institution, pp.17-18.

ment of an existing market, targeting a new region or age group, for example. The first firm in the market can capture market share without worrying about rivals. When competitors or imitators arrive, a likely event in knowledge-intensive fields with little patent or copyright protection like software, the first firm in will continue to have what are known as "first mover advantages": name recognition, the best marketing outlets, and a smoothly operating production and distribution system.

Once a particular set of procedures has been learned and accepted, users may continue to want to use it; this is known as a lock-in effect.[9] It may enable the first mover to establish some monopoly power by excluding or discouraging competitors. This is a powerful incentive for pioneering new technologies or marketing strategies.

On the other hand the innovator may not be successful. The costs of being a first mover are high. New technologies must not only be created but must be adapted to the market. New markets must be studied and appropriate marketing strategies formulated. Beginning a new operation from scratch has significant costs in areas like set up, publicity, and special offers.

Being a first mover is extremely risky. A majority of innovations do not succeed, even in large established companies. In the knowledge economy, the second mover, the imitator, has significant advantages. Experienced staff can be hired from the first mover, and they may have inside information. In any case, much technical information can be acquired, legally or illegally. Products can be reverse-engineered. Followers need not repeat all the learning mistakes made by the first mover, and may be able to tweak the product to performance beyond what the first mover has achieved. The new economy, with its heavy weighting toward knowledge-intensive fields, is thus likely to be a scene of active product competition.

STANDARDS

Standard-setting is one of the ways firms, often first movers, can build a monopoly position.

Many computer programs are linked to each other. Standards govern the interfaces between them. Numerous aspects of technical programming may be involved, such as how a video signal is treated or how an application links to the underlying operating system. The standards of an Apple computer are dif-

---

[9]The classic case is the QWERTY keyboard originally set up to prevent the keys jamming on a manual typewriter. Leibowitz has argued that what he calls the "weak" lock-in effect can be overcome if the quality of the new product sufficiently offsets the disadvantages of the old. His notion of a "strong" lock-in effect that depends on the fact that all users of a network must be on the same standard becomes less important as systems that can use various standards or are independent of a specific standard are introduced. Stan Leibowitz (2002). *Re-Thinking the Networked Economy.* New York: Amacom Press.

ferent from those of the Windows operating system and that means that Windows programs must be adapted to run on an Apple. There are also significant differences between different types of cellular phone systems.

The firm that sets the prevailing standard thus has significant advantages. With regard to applications, using a particular program often requires an extended learning period. To the extent that all programs in a suite of programs have the same look and feel (a common user interface), it is easy to move from one to the others.

Setting a standard that is widely accepted is a big marketing advantage. First movers sometimes can set the standard, though there have been many occasions when by improving on the first model later market entrants have been able to establish a new program standard. Control of the standard may be used as a barrier to the entry of competing firms. It may also be used to promote the sale of other goods. This is known as tying—forcing firms to use a particular application as a condition for the use of an operating system—or *bundling*—combining two products, which was the case with Microsoft Explorer and Windows (Case 11.1).

Finally, once companies have acquired substantial market power, they may be able to solidify or even expand their monopoly position for long periods. Many economists feel that Microsoft, the developer of the Windows operating system, has such advantages, some due to economies of scale, some the result of company practices. Microsoft has been able to maintain its commanding share of the operating system market and appears to be extending that monopoly into a variety of applications.

Paradoxically, setting standards may have important social benefits. It is easier to operate and interact on a network where there is a single standard rather than a multiplicity of different standards. For example, the use of a common GSM cell phone standard in Europe greatly facilitates the development and use of the European cell phone network. The social gains of a standard must be offset against the risks of monopoly or rigidity when a common standard applies.

Case 11.1
The Microsoft Antitrust Suit

Microsoft is the dominant producer of PC operating systems, with a 95 percent market share for Windows. It produces a number of important applications closely linked to its Windows system, among them Word, Excel, Powerpoint, Access, and Explorer.

Microsoft has been found by the courts to have a monopoly in the operating system business. That in itself is not a violation of the law, but the courts found Microsoft guilty of using its monopoly position to carry out anticompetitive practices in violation of the antitrust laws—tying contracts, predatory pricing, withholding of technical information, bundling—to prevent the growth of competition and to extend its monopoly to applications markets like browsers and word processing. The Department of Justice (DoJ) was particularly concerned with Microsoft's introduction of its Explorer browser and its substantially successful effort to eliminate the competing browser, Netscape. Microsoft bundled its Explorer with the Windows system, gave it away free, and instructed computer manufacturers not to use Windows unless Explorer was the default browser. Moreover, it would not permit manufacturers to alter the Windows opening screen to show the competing browser.

One idea of DoJ was to break up Microsoft into an operating systems company and an applications company. Another proposal was to impose limitations on Microsoft's behavior. It was difficult, however, to find behavioral remedies that would be enforceable to make sure that Microsoft did not continue its anticompetitive practices. Initially Justice Thomas Penfield Jackson found that Microsoft had a monopoly in operating systems, was using it to extend its monopoly into applications, and should be broken up, but his ruling was reversed on appeal.

Following the change of federal political administration in 2001, DoJ and Microsoft reached a consent agreement that would somewhat limit Microsoft's predatory activities. The agreement was widely considered a mere slap on the wrist. While it ordered Microsoft to make its Windows operating system available to all comers on equal terms, it did not require publication of the source code or even the sale of the Windows program bare of some of its built-in applications. Nine state governments refused to go along but their suit was largely rejected in 2002. Microsoft must still resolve outstanding charges before the European commission.

An interesting perspective on Microsoft was revealed recently when for the first time Microsoft broke down its profit statistics by division. The group responsible for Windows and its related applications had a profit margin of 85 percent, while other Microsoft operations, like entertainment, MSN Internet services, and business solutions, were running substantial deficits. The natural inference is that Microsoft has been using the extraordinary profits earned on its monopoly operating system to finance entry into other markets.

Many experts are concerned that the limited sanctions imposed will not prevent Microsoft from dominating the next generation of computer network operating systems and applications. Already Microsoft is attacking new worlds, among them smart phones for Web surfing and business management applications for small and medium-size companies. In the business applications market Microsoft is building links between its accounting programs, which have lots of competition, to its Office spreadsheet programs.

Microsoft has not been so successful extending its monopoly into advanced phones, where Nokia is fighting back, and into server programs, where some firms are turning to Linux in order not to be dependent on Microsoft. The only hope in general, however, is that rapid technical changes may make operating systems a contestable market.

INFORMATION ECONOMICS: CLOSED AND OPEN SYSTEMS

Knowledge has value. In dynamic, technically changing fields like IT, new ideas are central to establishing and maintaining a competitive market position. Some developments can be patented as new methods or inventions, so high-tech firms have been filing patent applications at an unprecedented rate. In fields like pharmaceuticals, where a single patent may cover all aspects of a drug, patents help to establish and maintain a temporary, and sometimes a not so temporary, monopoly position.

In the IT industries the situation is somewhat different. Patents on hardware may apply to both designs and processes, and their use is licensed to manufacturers. IBM earns more than $2 billion a year from licensing fees.

For software, some programs related to products and processes can also be patented. In most cases, software is protected not by patent but by copyright laws, which apply for a much longer period. Software makers can also treat their source code as confidential and seek protection under trade secrets legislation.

Software copyright protection applies to the specific code in a software program. This does not protect copyright owners from someone using different code to accomplish the same result. Moreover, violation of fair use provisions of the copyright law that permit free private use is frequent in the United States. Abroad, particularly in the developing countries, software piracy and the unlicensed reproduction of music CDs and video DVDs are rampant. China, where copied CDs and DVDs can be bought openly on the street for the equivalent of U.S. $1.00, promised to provide some intellectual property protection as part of its effort to become a member of the World Trade Organization (WTO), but there is widespread concern that the new regulations will not be enforced.

The information embodied in a program is often very important if a firm is to earn continuing income from its programming efforts, protect a market niche, or even establish a monopoly position, but protecting intellectual software property is sometimes difficult. Moreover, there are cases where making the information widely available may be very important for expanding application of a software product. For example, the developer of a computer language may want to facilitate its use by other firms to build application programs.

The two common approaches to disseminating software are the closed code and the open code approaches. Closed code means that the source code written in machine language is kept secret. A firm may license users but provide them only with the specific information required by application engineers. This is the Microsoft Windows model.

In the open code approach the idea is that widespread availability of the source code in the worldwide community of programmers will encourage its further improvement and its use. The source code is not necessarily free to all users but it is available in a form that can be read and understood. Linux (Case 11.2) is the classic example of an open code approach and there are numerous other open code applications.

The choice between closed code and open code approaches has often been seen as a matter of social philosophy, but there are sound economic explanations. Intellectual property is valuable only to the extent that it can be sold or translated into salable products. An established firm, particularly one dominating a market, will choose a closed code approach; its computer code is of great value and presumably is already widely integrated into applications programs. On the other hand, a newcomer or a firm seeking to break into an established market may benefit from the open code approach if it serves to further enhance the new material and its applications.

Case 11.2
Linux and the Open Code Movement

What is Linux? It is an operating system that was written by a student, Linus Torvalds, in his Helsinki room in 1991. In contrast to the procedure with similar systems, Torvalds made the source code widely available under a general public license. He claims that he neither planned to make a profit nor had any grand political or economic designs. The idea was that programmers worldwide would expand the program, make it more user-friendly, and adapt it for their specialized purposes.

The program is not always free. Developers like Red Hat may charge for their versions, which have been adapted for easier installation and come with an instruction manual, so long as the basic source code remains available. The Linux operating system, which is based on Unix, is said to be remarkably stable and adaptable.

As a pioneering effort, Linux has had considerable success. Many contributors have helped to expand the program and to provide applications for it. Many versions are now widely and cheaply available. Even large computer companies like IBM and Sun are lending their support, perhaps as a way of countering Microsoft's Windows. Other firms, too, have begun to follow the open source model, encouraging free expanded use of their proprietary software. On the other hand, Microsoft Windows remains the dominant operating system by far.

Few PC users have made the transition to Linux. It is not yet user-friendly or advantageous enough to persuade the average computer user to replace Windows. But some major corporations are migrating to Linux servers to take advantage of low-cost open-source data management software. The future of Linux may lie in enterprise applications and in its use in dedicated operating systems for specialized Web appliances, cell phones, even cars. This is where an open system like Linux that can be modified to optimize its application has special advantages.

ENTREPRENEURSHIP AND INDUSTRIAL ORGANIZATION

An entrepreneurial culture has played a significant role in the development of IT industries in the United States. In the beginning the computer revolution was in the hands of small companies, started like Apple Computer in a garage or like Microsoft in a bedroom. While the laboratories of giant firms like IBM, ATT, and Xerox were responsible for some of the most important technical developments—like the integrated circuit, the computer desktop presentation, and the mouse—these firms were not successful at exploiting their ideas commercially.

This is true for both hardware and software. Many of the firms responsible for the applications that lie behind the e-revolution were startups. An astonishing entrepreneurial culture thrived in regional clusters like Silicon Valley, Seattle, Austin, and Boston around new high-tech firms in software, digital electronics, and biotechnology. Most of the leaders of the e-revolution were very young, often under 30, some coming from graduate departments at major universities but others moving into CEO positions before they had finished their undergraduate or business school programs.

They were long on dreams but short on practical experience. While some of them became spectacular successes and very rich, many others failed or were replaced by more mature and more experienced business managers. The 2001 recession turned out to be a shakeout period. Many firms failed as their revenue or profit projections could not be met. Many were closed down; some were absorbed by larger, more successful competitors.

A few of the startups have become huge businesses themselves, displacing some of the older giants or merging with them. Today, many competitors have been squeezed out of business. We think of Microsoft as a giant firm doing everything it can think of to maintain its dominant position in operating systems (Windows) and trying to extend its stranglehold onto other related functions like browsers and word processors. Its ability to do so reflects economies of scale, first mover advantages, an enormous cash flow, and a worldwide scope. Few smaller companies can prevail against giant firms like that.

If past history is any guide, the large dominant firms of today may not be the ones that make or apply path-breaking developments. Today's giant firms, too, may be displaced by the next generation of IT innovators.

ENTREPRENEURSHIP AND FINANCIAL CONSIDERATIONS

High-tech startups have been greatly facilitated by important financial innovations, though these have been drastically affected by the crash of high-tech stocks in the 2000-2001 period.

In the past, small-scale entrepreneurs were limited in their ability to get capital. In Europe and Japan, this is still a huge barrier. In the 1990s in the United States, venture capitalists financed many of the new dot-com companies. For the successful dot-coms the payoff has been large indeed.

The typical venture capital firm does a great deal more than provide initial seed capital. The budding entrepreneur must begin by preparing a business plan outlining what is proposed. Such a prospectus includes an evaluation of the market opportunity, a discussion of the personnel team, and a summary of company strategy for production and marketing: How does the proposed firm plan to differentiate itself from the competition? A detailed financial plan projecting revenues and costs lies at the heart of the proposal. This kind of plan, which probably contains as much imagination as reality, becomes the basis for the initial financial commitment and for setting benchmarks against which future performance can be judged.

Venture capital investors like to see companies with a finished product, established customers, and a large expanding market, but most new visionary companies are far from this target. As a result, venture capital firms have taken on an important role as incubators. For extended periods they guide the operations of the new firms, often helping to select managerial talent, guiding strategy decisions, and establishing an appropriate managerial culture. A small financial stake at the beginning of a business has multiplied many times by the time the firm goes public. On the other hand, more recently many e-ventures and dot-coms have collapsed as they failed to make their guideline targets, running out of cash before they began to make a profit—in some extreme cases, even before they took in any revenue.

Initial public offerings (IPOs) have been a favorite mechanism to translate entrepreneurial effort into large profits. When a new firm is sufficiently mature to go public, the IPO is often sold at a discount from the estimated market value of the shares. The result is that the early participants make huge profits when the IPO is made. Holders of stock options, another favorite way to reward senior management, also make a killing as stock prices are inflated. It goes almost without saying that IPOs have become very rare indeed in the current post-dot-com crash world.

Junk bond markets also helped to provide capital for risky firms early on, but, as with IPOs, these sources of funds are fragile. They dry up as soon as there is a loss of confidence, as happened in 2001.

GROWTH THEORY AND EVOLUTIONARY ECONOMICS

We now turn to theory, to a concern with the economy as a whole. What do economists have to say about innovation and growth? Traditional economic growth theory contrasts quite sharply with evolutionary economics. Can these two views be reconciled in terms of the e-business revolution?

The theory of economic growth has not been helpful in explaining the e-business phenomenon. The original production function-based approach[10] introduces technological change as a residual after explaining growth in terms of the impact of labor and capital inputs. The approach translates into the following formula in growth rate terms, relating output to inputs and to a technological change factor called total factor productivity (TFP):

TFP growth = Output growth - (Contribution of labor and capital inputs to growth)

This can be measured as:

% change in TFP = % change in GDP - (a * % change in labor + (1-a) * % change in capital),

where the weight "a" corresponds to the share of labor in total GDP and the weight "(1-a)" is the capital share.[11]

We call productivity computed in this way *total factor productivity* because it represents the improvement in productivity that accrues to all production factors. However, since it is calculated as a residual, it has no simple explanation. Though it is usually referred to as technical change, in practice it may include not just changes in technology but also improvements in manage-

---

[10]Robert M. Solow (1957). "Technical Change and the Aggregate Production Function." *Review of Economics and Statistics,* 39: 312-20.

[11]For a discussion, see Robert M. Solow (1989). *Growth Theory: An Exposition.* New York: Oxford University Press. The approach makes certain narrow but critical assumptions that may not square with reality. For example, it assumes (a) diminishing returns: the marginal productivity of a production factor declines as more of it is used relative to other factors, (b) a competitive economy where production factors are paid their marginal products, and (c) a production process that maintains constant returns to scale.

ment, economies of scale, and even negative elements like the cost of environmental pollution.[12] In other words, in the attempt to measure technical change, we have taken away the meaning of the term; we have indeed thrown out the baby with the bathwater.

Traditional growth theory visualizes technical change as occurring independent of the inputs into production—using a more capital-intensive production process does not alter technology and does not add to TFP. More recent theories of economic growth, on the other hand, allow explicitly for the production and utilization of knowledge, usually measured as human capital. But again there is little explanation of what knowledge is and how it is used productively.

Finally, the endogenous growth theories[13] recognize that knowledge interacts with other production factors and from the perspective of society it may not have diminishing returns. Knowledge is incorporated into the productive power of new machinery and into the abilities of workers. Knowledge developed and used by one innovator remains available to society as a whole, becoming a basis for building further knowledge. Such a view fits the IT/e-business revolution much better than previous theories.

In the real world, new knowledge like that incorporated into business applications of IT is introduced in a series of stages. We visualize the following:

- *Invention.* The initial new idea. It may be a sophisticated technical development that originates in the research laboratories of large corporations or universities or it may be a much simpler brainstorm occurring in somebody's study or backyard.

- *Innovation.* Turning the idea into a commercially viable product. In the process, the invention may have been patented but, perhaps surprisingly, some of the new developments in the IT fields do not meet the requirements for patents. As we have noted, software is often not patented but is kept secret or covered by the copyright laws.

- *Experience.* A great deal of progress is simply the result of the experience of producing and using a new product—another aspect of "learning by doing." The new product must be adapted to the needs of its users. It takes time before the features of a technically complex product are simplified sufficiently for popular application. And it takes practice before users are fully accustomed to its use.

---

[12]The attempt to break down the residual is often referred to as "growth accounting;" see Edward F. Denison. *Accounting for US Economic Growth.* Washington: Brookings, 1974. But such a calculation remains quite arbitrary.

[13]Paul Romer (1986). "Increasing Returns and Long-Run Growth." *Journal of Political Economy,* 94: 1002-37.

- *Diffusion.* The dispersion of the new product from its originator to the market. Some products can be adopted widely and quickly but others may take some time to be diffused. That has been one of the difficulties faced by e-business products that rely on fast broadband transmission, which has not been adopted as rapidly as had been expected.

The process of acquiring knowledge and putting it to work does involve traditional economic mechanisms like savings and investment. It recognizes that new technologies are usually associated with the acquisition of new capital, whether that is hard or soft. It may also imply that it may take time before the new machinery or new software introduced will affect productivity.

A somewhat more descriptive, and perhaps more accurate, view of technical progress, the evolutionary approach, takes these considerations into account and places them in the context of business competition and rivalry.[14] Schumpeter's notions of product differentiation and creative destruction fit into this category.[15] Evolutionary economists reject some of the simplifications of traditional theorists, replacing them with the concept of an evolving socio-business world. Inventions and innovations are motivated not simply by profit maximization but also by broader social objectives. In place of a representative firm, there are business strategists at different stages, some young upstarts and others more experienced, and probably more rigid, in mature large firms.

Development and growth in the IT fields and related e-businesses are evolutionary. Business evolution is likely to be episodic rather than smooth. There may be long periods with little change, then suddenly advanced versions of products are introduced with astonishing rapidity. Sometimes they come from existing firms; sometimes they reflect the competitive activity of new entrants. There is a great deal of turmoil in the flexible dynamic stage (in which many aspects of IT still remain). This makes it very difficult to predict in which directions new economy industries will go—but we can be certain that there is a great deal of movement yet to come.

ECONOMIC DEVELOPMENT AND E-BUSINESS

Growth theory applies to developing as well as to advanced economies. There are, however, some crucial differences—besides the basic one that the advanced countries have higher incomes. Economic development can be seen as a process of transition from a primitive economy to an advanced modern economy. Many developing countries have some high points of development in their urban sectors characterized by good education, modern financial systems, high-tech com-

---

[14]For a discussion, see R. R. Nelson and S. G. Winter (1982). *An Evolutionary Theory of Economic Change.* Cambridge, MA: Harvard University Press.
[15]Joseph Schumpeter (1975). *Capitalism, Socialism, and Democracy.* New York: Harper.

munication, etc., but large parts of the society lag behind in rural, often primitive, self-sufficient agriculture. Development in that situation, means moving an ever-larger fraction of the population from the primitive to the modern economy, which often means a transition from the rural into the urban sector.

It is a happy fact that in the past few decades many countries have succeeded at economic development. In East Asia in particular, even populous countries like China are moving toward advanced-country status. However, most of them are still a long way from the level of educational and technical achievement that we observe in Western Europe, the United States, and Japan.

As we have pointed out, economic growth calls for accumulation of capital and knowledge technology. For economic development, the fact that knowledge and technology are available from more advanced countries has been a big help. We speak of *imitative development:* Developing countries can learn the techniques used by more advanced countries. The growth of advanced industries and management are a cornerstone of most countries' economic development strategies.

Some countries propose to go a step further by leapfrogging: In the effort to advance technology, a country may skip some stages of technological development altogether, leapfrogging over them. A good example of this is the rapid acceptance of mobile phone service in many developing countries. Since national telecoms had failed to provide adequate land-line service, many consumers simply went directly to the more sophisticated and more economic cellular phones. Similar possibilities are DVD video disks instead of VCRs, debit and credit cards in place of checks, and e-commerce in place of traditional trading. For example, Lawrence Lau writes, "China has the ability to leapfrog—there are no vested interests to protect; no existing businesses to be cannibalized; there can be 'creation without destruction.'"[16]

That view may be on the optimistic side. Even in China, there are businesses with strong vested interests. Indeed, government ownership or support of firms in some important sectors may stand in the way of importing sophisticated e-business systems. Many observers fear that will happen in banking and related financial services, even though China has promised to open them to foreign competition as part of its deal to enter the WTO.

Moreover, the high level of educational and technological support and the concentration of suppliers required by advanced technology and its application in e-commerce may make leapfrogging difficult. IT-related development may not be appropriate at this time for countries that lack sufficient infrastructure and education. After all, it has not been possible for Indonesia to build an aircraft indus-

---

[16]Lawrence J. Lau (2000). "The New Chinese Economy: A View from the Outside." *<http://www.stanford.edu/~ljlau>*.

try, and there is still uncertainty about whether Malaysia's state-created automobile industry will ever be economically viable. Still, certain more advanced East Asian countries like Taiwan, South Korea, and Singapore are having considerable success by specializing in important segments of the new IT hardware market. Singapore in particular sees its future in the knowledge economy.

The question is whether e-business represents a way for developing economies in general to make a quick step into the advanced world. As we will consider further later, that may be easier for specialized high-tech production that can be organized by foreign investors than for e-commerce, which calls for broad changes in commercial practice. But there are many new possibilities. Regions that are ambitious enough to attempt the arduous climb to higher technological or managerial heights should not be discouraged from making the attempt.

Chapter 12
Economic Impact of E-Business

What has been the economic impact of the e-business revolution? Does the revolution imply a reorganization of business organization and structure? How does it affect sectors of the economy and its aggregate performance?

First we will discuss the relationship between e-business and globalization. Then we will discuss measuring the impact of e-business at the firm and sector level. Finally we will consider the impact from the perspective of the economy as a whole.

GLOBALIZATION AND E-BUSINESS

Globalization is an important aspect of the new economy, but cynics will note that integration of the world economy has been going on for many years. World trade and international capital flows have been growing for a long time. Is there a connection between increasing globalization and e-business?

Globalization is far from a new development. International commerce between East and West goes back to the 15th-century spice traders, though we do better to focus on the rapid expansion of international specialization and trade after World War II. Some of the growth of trade and international capital flows must be attributed to reduced tariff barriers and financial liberalization. Transportation costs have also been declining steadily for years. More important, perhaps, is that shipping from a producing country to the market takes far less time today than it used to—what used to take three months to ship across the ocean can now be shipped by containership in 10 days and even more rapidly (though not as cheaply) by air. That has made possible international specialization and the migration of mass-production industries to the low-labor-cost countries in East Asia.

The process of international interaction is accelerating. Now it is not just trade in goods but more and more flows of capital and information services. Much of the payoff has been positive, though some results, like unemployment or low wages among unskilled workers in advanced countries and the increasing volatility of international capital flows and exchange rates, are cause for concern.

How much of this represents e-business or one of its effects? International retail e-commerce (B2C), consumers ordering directly from abroad over the Internet, remains minuscule. The problems of fulfillment still make international consumer e-business difficult: how to manage shipping, customs clearance, returns? Some products like software or music, though, are suited for electronic transmission internationally.

International B2B e-commerce between producers abroad and marketers at home is much more promising. Once foreign contacts have been established, electronic communication greatly speeds up business transactions. Orders, shipment control, and payments can be carried out instantaneously, even if the supplier is on the other side of the world. Physical operations, like setting up an international affiliate or building a plant abroad, still require site visits and direct personal negotiations by business representatives, but these may be one time or infrequent occurrences while routine transactions are carried on electronically.

Electronic communication channels have become central in managing some international ventures. Cisco Systems in Costa Rica, for example, has set up its own satellite communications system to headquarters and other company locations in order to improve both bandwidth and reliability over the telecom service that would otherwise be available. There is no doubt that international electronic communication helps to facilitate linkages between countries and to speed up the transmission of knowledge between them. (As I write this paragraph, I am in Nanjing, China. The text will be stored on my home computer system in Boston, from where I can retrieve it at any time for corrections.)

BUSINESS PRACTICE AND ORGANIZATION

Anecdotal evidence demonstrates the large impact of network computerization on the corporate organization and success of individual firms. After firms buy the basic computers and programming required, they must make huge investments in organizational learning and these often require innovative approaches. Many firms have spent millions of dollars to reconfigure their operations to take advantage of computer connections with suppliers and customers. Such changes in work practices have been documented in numerous case studies of

IT adoption.[1] In some cases, these changes have been enormously successful; in others, they have been difficult to absorb; in still others, they have been abandoned.

The Internet alone has had large effects on business practice, making possible a broad reorganization of how businesses communicate and how they are managed.

Empirical evidence suggests that restructuring prompted by the introduction of computer-based operations is skill-biased toward workers with more training and better skills. One explanation for this is that computers are more likely to substitute for workers in functions that call for standardized rule-based procedures, thus placing relatively greater emphasis on human judgment and decision-making where that continues to be required. The complexity of high-tech equipment also calls for more-qualified workers as operations are computerized. Firm-level empirical studies suggest that skill bias reflects the combination of information technology with complementary workplace reorganization and new products and services.[2]

Tripplet presents an interesting example of the interrelations between computerization and organization on a global level:

"Suppose a not so hypothetical toy company that once manufactured toys in the United States. The computer, and faster and cheaper telecommunications through the Internet, has made it possible to operate a toy business in a globally integrated way. Today, the company's head office (in the U.S.) determines what toys are likely to sell in the United States, designs the toys, and plans the marketing campaign and the distribution of toys. But it contracts all toy manufacturing to companies in Asia, which might not be affiliated with the U.S. company in any ownership way. When the toys are completed, they are shipped directly from the Asian manufacturer to large

---

[1]Larry W. Hunter, et al. (2000). "It's Not Just the ATMs: Firm Strategies, Work Restructuring and Workers' Earnings in Retail Banking" Unpublished. Philadelphia: Wharton School; Frank Levy et al. (2000). "Computerization and Skills: Examples from a Car Dealership." Unpublished. Cambridge, MA: MIT; Richard J. Murnane, et al. (1999). "Technological Change, Computers, and Skill Demands: Evidence from Back Office Operations of a Large Bank." Presented at the NBER Labor Workshop, Cambridge, MA; and Erik Brynjolfsson and Lorin M. Hitt (2000). "Beyond Computation: Information Technology, Organizational Transformation, and Business Performance." *Journal of Economic Perspectives,* 14 (4): 23-48; *<http://ebusiness.mit.edu/erik>*.

[2]Levy et al., op. cit., no. 1; Murnane et al., op. cit., no. 1; Timothy F. Bresnahan et al. (2002). "Information Technology, Workplace Organization, and the Demand for Skilled Labor: Firm-Level Evidence." *Quarterly Journal of Economics,* 117: 339-76, *<http:// ebusiness.mit.edu/erik>*.

U.S. toy retailers; thus, this U.S. toy company has no direct substantial U.S. wholesale arm either. The billing and financial transactions are handled in some offshore financial center, perhaps in the Bahamas. The computer and advanced information technology have made it possible for this company to locate the activities of manufacturing, distribution, financial record-keeping and so forth in different parts of the world where costs are lowest."[3]

Reich provides a similar example, more focused on the Internet: *"Micro-businesses hire Web designers to set up sites and pay an Internet service provider a monthly fee to house them; rent software for ordering and billing; contract for shipping and delivery; rent a secure server line for credit card transactions, and have a bank manage them. If such businesses need it, they can tap into a global reservoir of expertise. They can find all these services on the Internet, where they find their customers as well."[4]*

Such virtual enterprises would not have been possible in an earlier era.

We may summarize some of the changes in business management and organization that are related to the reduced cost and increased speed of communication and transactions that is central to the e-business revolution:

- Supplies and parts may be sourced more widely and products may be distributed to markets that are farther away.
  –Firms may seek a broader range of suppliers, increasing competition.
  –Firms may more easily produce abroad, as in the toy example.
  –Distribution may be direct with fewer or no branch outlets.
  –Entire business functions like management information systems and accounting may be outsourced.

- Inventory control may be automated and may be tighter when mathematical optimization is used to manage the production process.

- Industry structure may also change.
  –To take advantage of economies of scale, firms may become larger, often by acquiring competitors.
  –On the other hand, there may be more room for firms that offer finely specialized niche services.

---

[3]Jack E. Tripplet (1999). "The Solow Productivity Paradox: What Do Computers Do to Productivity?" *Canadian Journal of Economics,* 32 (2): 309-34.
[4]Robert B. Reich (2002). *The Future of Success.* New York: Random House, Vintage Books, p. 19.

MICROECONOMIC EFFECTS ON PRODUCTIVITY

How is the economic impact of e-business manifested?

The discussion must begin with a look at its impact on productivity. The objective of an e-business innovation—a new computerized ordering system, for example—is to reduce costs, improve convenience, or perhaps capture market share. From the perspective of the measured growth of the economy, the critical issue is cost reduction or efficiency improvement.

Are e-businesses more productive? Since these businesses are a form of automation, an increase in productivity might be expected. A task, the sale and shipment of a book, for example, that used to require the services of a salesperson is now done electronically without human intervention. Inventory control and ordering is also automated, and is now better linked to real-time purchasing. Just-in-time inventories become a reality.

For the bookseller, there are gains in the productivity of both labor and capital (though these may be offset by vastly increased costs of computer programming and operation). Improved productivity may show up first in the bookseller's profits. Ultimately, if the gain is competed away as other firms also adopt improved practices, the consumer will benefit from the lower price of books. The national accounts will measure this gain as a reduction in the price deflator and, assuming a constant nominal GDP, as an increase in real GDP.

Similar gains will be possible at all stages of the supply chain for manufacturing industries. This is where the productivity improvements as a result of networked IT are likely to be greatest.

Tripplet[5] follows the toy manufacturer example already quoted by asking where the gains in productivity will show up. The new virtual organization may have led to vast increases in profits for toy company stockholders and management, but while there may have been gains in productivity abroad, perhaps for the Asian manufacturers, only the head office is left in the United States. Though the output of the head office, specifically its contribution to the productivity of the overseas operations, may have been substantial, it is not well measured—indeed, it may not be measured at all.

Some of these gains may trickle down to the final purchaser. As we have noted, the consumer may also see other gains that are not measured in the national accounts. Among these are the vast quantities of information available through the Web, the improvements in consumer choice, and the increased convenience of many Internet-linked operations.

---

[5]Tripplett, op. cit., no. 3.

Case 12.1
Some Personal Computer Experiences

The huge unmeasured gains associated with computer networks are illustrated by the following personal examples:

- When I travel abroad, I am in constant e-mail contact with my family. Even video conversations are possible, though the quality is still not entirely satisfactory. The value of these contacts was brought home to me last summer when I was temporarily out of reach of the e-mail network; even the local cybercafé was not operating. I felt completely isolated. It was hard to imagine being so reliant on a method of communications that became available only a few years ago.

- The text of this book was typed using a voice recognition system. That works quite well, although occasionally it can make embarrassing mistakes. If you use that kind of system, be sure to read over the text before you print it! But mistakes and all, it is better than repeated typing.

- In an earlier chapter when I was referring to Moore's law, I thought I needed more information. Instead of going to the library, I simply entered the words "Moore's law" into my search engine. In less than a minute, I had all the information I wanted on my screen.

Professor Robert Gordon[6] has asked whether the gains that we can make from business automation are anywhere near as large as those that were obtained in previous industrial revolutions, when, for example, the steam engine or the electric motor was introduced. I believe they are. The contribution of networked computers may be somewhat different from the introduction of labor-saving machinery, but it is important.

In the industrial revolution, the introduction of large machines supplanted the hand labor of many workers; this is called substitution of capital for labor. Today, automated interaction over a computer system sometimes many miles away is replacing human interaction, much of which often took place directly between one person and another. Brad DeLong of the University of California says, "IT and the Internet amplify brain power in the same way that the technologies of the industrial revolution amplified muscle power."[7] Each individual transaction may save only a small amount of time, but when there are

---

[6]Robert J. Gordon (2000). "Does the 'New Economy' Measure Up to the Great Inventions of the Past?" *Journal of Economic Perspectives*, 4 (14): 40-74
[7]*The Economist*, 2000. <*http://www.economist.com*>.

many, many transactions the labor-saving is astonishing, especially considering how many people are engaged in communications and negotiations simply to make our economic system operate: salespeople, accountants, order fillers, telephone-response people, insurance agents and stockbrokers, record clerks, and so on. That 20 percent or more of the labor force is engaged in these tasks is not an unreasonable estimate. Not all of them can be replaced by a computer or a voice recognition system, but even if only one in five were to be replaced by electronic equipment, that could potentially free 4 percent of the labor force for other activities. That in turn would significantly reduce costs and increase potential GDP. It is not a good idea to underestimate the potential gains just because they are not directly concerned with physical activity.

DIFFUSION OF INNOVATIONS

As with earlier industrial revolutions, it takes a long time before an innovation is diffused throughout the economy. At first, only a few potential users may experiment with a new product or program. Once the product or program is perfected and becomes widely known, it may be diffused rapidly for a time, but ultimately diffusion will slow. The S-curve of diffusion, sometimes stretching over many years, may explain why gains from e-commerce have been so long in coming.

Moreover, it takes time until the new technologies are fully integrated into production procedures. A productivity and growth accounting study of 600 firms shows that computers together with investments in organizational form make a positive contribution to output growth, not instantly but within one to seven years.[8] The gains in productivity we have seen in recent years as a result of increased application of network technology reflect technological innovations that occurred many years earlier.

Figure 12.1 illustrates the gradual diffusion of technical innovations in the U. S. economy. In comparison with some past technical revolutions, the diffusion of cellular phones and home computers has been quite rapid; they went from minimal to widespread use in less than a decade. The speed of diffusion reflects in part the extraordinarily rapid decline in the cost of computation and communication.

There is still room for further expansion of the use of PCs and Internet connections. Figure 12.2 shows the rapid diffusion of computers and Internet access in the United States in the 1990s. By 2000, about half of U.S. households had computers and almost all of them had Internet access, though it was

---

[8]Shinkyu Yang and E. Brynjolffson (2001). "Intangible Assets and Growth Accounting." Unpublished research paper; <*http://ebusiness.mit.edu/erik*>.

probably still slow. Fast broadband access, which requires cable or DSL equipment, lags much further behind. It is not expanding as rapidly as had been expected because its cost remains high.

Figure 12.1: Technological Diffusion

Household adoption of selected technologies since 1900. The rapid adoption of computers and cellular phones today has its parallel in earlier technologies.

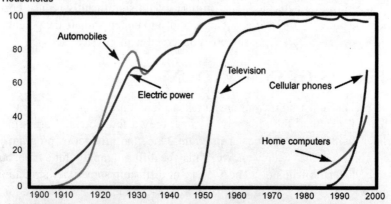

Note: Automobile and cellular phone adoptions are estimated by dividing the number of registrations and subscriptions by the number of U.S. households. These numbers will overstate actual adoption when households register multiple cars or purchase multiple cellular subscriptions.

Source: Robert J. Gordon (2000), "Does the 'New Economy' Measure Up to the Great Inventions of the Past?" *Journal of Economic Perspectives,* 4 (14): 40-74.

Figure 12.2: Diffusion Curve for Computers

U.S. households with computers and Internet access: Selected years

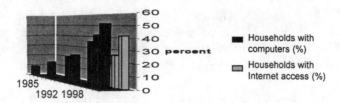

Source: World Bank Development Indicators Data.

Though computer access provides a basis for E-commerce, these figures do not show how much the computers were used for networked business purposes. Much business computer use still relies on proprietary intracompany systems. Networked Internet use for business purposes has plenty of room for expansion, though there are undoubtedly great differences between sectors and between firms within a sector. Many people believe that the e-business revolution has only just begun, that many more applications can be developed and implemented. In that case, we are only at an early stage of the diffusion curve for many IT innovations.

SPEEDING UP THE PRODUCT CYCLE

The product cycle is the period of time typically seen between the introduction of new products and the appearance of newer products. If we look at the product cycle in terms of a broad class of equipment, digital electronics, for example, the cycle might take a very long time. On the other hand, if we look at it in terms of model change, new versions of existing machines, that might take only a year or two—recently, the time might even be measured in months.

The brevity of the product cycle is a good indicator of the speed of technical change. Some observers have made an important point of the fact that the product cycle, the time it takes to bring out new products, appears to have speeded up recently. This speedup would tend to increase the rate of productivity growth, though only while the speedup is taking place. Once the speed of product development has stabilized again, the rate of productivity growth would again be where scientific progress and innovation investment would put it.

There is evidence, though, that the innovation cycle has become shorter. An extreme example is that makers of chips have been introducing new generations of products every six months. Is this reduction in the time for producing new products related to the e-business revolution? That is not entirely clear.

One explanation is that the increased pace of innovation and product development may simply reflect old-fashioned competition among chipmakers. For this, the stage of evolution of the technology may be an important consideration. In the philosophy of science, as new developments overthrow normal science in the sense described by Thomas Kuhn,[9] when a breakthrough to a new technology is made, a plethora of new possibilities suddenly becomes available. Similarly, as new information technology replaces older modes of communication, many more IT and e-business developments become feasible and are introduced quickly.

The potential for innovations is far from exhausted. In testimony to Congress in July 2002, Federal Reserve Chairman Greenspan commented on

[9]Thomas S. Kuhn (1962). *The Structure of Scientific Revolutions.* Chicago: University of Chicago Press.

recent investment surveys in which business managers were asked how large a share of available new IT developments their firms had already introduced. Invariably, year after year, the response was the same: "About 50 percent." Greenspan concluded that potential innovations were increasing as fast as innovations were being put in place.

Finally, the capabilities of modern computers and of communication may accelerate the process of developing new products. In the automobile industry, for example, computers can be used to quickly produce mockups of new car designs that earlier would have had to be drawn and manufactured by hand at great expense and over a substantial time period. There are ways in which the new technologies can be seen as speeding up the product innovation cycle.

ADVANTAGES OF E-BUSINESS FOR FIRMS

For the firm operating at the microeconomic level, the principal gains from e-business are increased efficiency of managing the order, production, inventory, and delivery cycle. These are measurable gains in that they improve productivity and reduce production cost.

Other advantages come from improved price-setting—more information is available. There are fewer differences between the information available to the seller and to the buyer and there is a wider range of competitors. This means that prices can be determined more accurately and faster.

Firms have also discovered that the range of competition is considerably broader. Instead of a few local suppliers, firms can now draw on materials and supplies offered by many sellers often from far away. This can significantly reduce the cost of supplies.

Finally, there is the problem of technology-based monopolies. Firms can take advantage of their leadership position in some technologies to dominate the market and, perhaps, to exclude potential competitors.

MERGERS AND ACQUISITIONS AND E-BUSINESS

We have already noted in Chapter 11 how the e-business revolution in altering transaction costs may lead to changes in business structure. Looking at U.S. economic history, the introduction of the electric motor is an interesting example of how far-reaching a narrow technical change can be (Case 12.2). Yet, the effects of the computer network are likely to be very different from a narrower development like a new source of power. The e-commerce revolution may have effects on business structure that are far broader, instigating a reorganization of how businesses communicate and how they are managed.

A reflection of the changes in business structure that have been taking place is an enormous increase in merger and acquisition activity in recent years. It is not clear, of course, the extent to which these mergers are rational responses to production-cost economies related to a larger scale of e-business or IT operations. They may well be. On the other hand, mergers could also be a way of realizing the potential profitability of a new venture by selling it at a high price. After the dot-com crash, we now know that some of these profit expectations were unrealistic. A third possibility is that mergers may be a way of capturing a larger market share that enhances a firm's ability to set prices or that may even give it monopoly power.

Case 12.2
The Electric Motor and Business Organization

The introduction of the electric motor was used by economic historian Paul David[10] to illustrate the technological learning curve, how far-reaching a technical change can be, and how long it can take before it significantly improves productivity.

Factories used to be organized around a central power source, usually water power or a large coal-driven steam engine. Because everything was connected by leather belts, it was necessary to cluster machines around the central power source. The vertical drive shaft from the power source accounted for the height of the brick factory buildings that still stand near rivers in smaller cities and towns in New England.

Electric motors were introduced in the 1880s. Initially, the power generated by these large electric motors was still conveyed to lathes, drills, presses, and other equipment by complex systems of shafts and belts. The machines requiring the most power were placed close to the power source; those calling for less power were located farther away. This was economical for conserving power but it made the factory floor inefficient. Materials and products had to be moved from machine to machine, from factory floor to factory floor, often in an illogical sequence.

As smaller, cheaper electric motors were invented, factory owners turned to unit drive—one motor for each machine. Drive shafts and belts were ripped out. The small electric motor made it possible to reorganize the factory floor. Production was spread out horizontal-

---

[10]Paul David (1991). "The Dynamo and the Computer: An Historical Perspective on the Modern Productivity Paradox." *American Economic Review Papers and Proceedings,* 1990, pp. 355-60.

ly and sequentially, making the modern assembly line possible. Factories could be located anywhere across the country even if water power or a coal supply were not available.

Though the cost of electric power gradually declined, many firms continued to use the old equipment until it wore out. As a result, it was almost 40 years before electric motors were broadly used and businesses had learned how to take full advantage of them. When they did, the result was a productivity boom in the 1920s.

Economists have argued about the transformation implied by IT. Its introduction has been equally complex and at first took time, though in recent years progress has been very fast. First, there were mainframe computers. Then came PCs. These were standalone units, unable to communicate with each another, often drawing on unique programming systems. It was not until computers were connected by the Internet and until data interchange between different systems became possible that e-mail and e-business became viable options. We are still in the middle of that technological transformation.

SAVINGS FROM E-DISTRIBUTION

Technological change is extremely rapid in the microelectronic hardware and software programming fields, but the real gains to come may be in the applications—the use of computer network automation to carry out tasks that heretofore have required human contact, pencil and paper.

Cost Reductions

Some of the cost reductions attributable to new Web-based approaches are readily visible—and they are spectacular (Table 12.1). In most cases, these reduced costs reflect the elimination of sales personnel or agent commissions. The level of service being provided to the customer may not be greatly reduced, though often the burden of searching for information and filling in the order blank falls on the customer.

Table 12.1: Costs under Old and IT Systems

	Old	Electronic
Airline ticket	$8	$1
Bill payment	$2-3	$0.60-1
Term life insurance	$400-700	$200-350
Software	$15	$0.20-0.50
Banking Transaction	$1.44	$0.04

Sources: Booz, Allen & Hamilton. OECD, *Electronic Impact of Electronic Commerce.*

It is not easy, however, to estimate the cost reductions that can be anticipated at the sector level when an entire industry switches to e-commerce. Table 12.2 shows estimates by industry, using input-output data from the staff

Table 12.2: Cost Savings from B2B Switch to E-Commerce

Industry	Cost Saving
Aerospace	11%
Chemicals	10%
Coal	2%
Communications	5-15%
Computing	11-20%
Electrical components	20-30%
Food	3-5%
Forest products	15-25%
Freight transport	15-20%
Healthcare	5%
Life sciences	12-19%
Machining	20%
Media and advertising	10-15%
Oil and gas	5-15%
Paper	10%
Steel	11%

Sources: Martin Brookes and Z. Wahhaj. "The Shocking Economic Effect of B2B." Goldman Sachs Global Economics Paper No. 37, February 3, 2000; and Gavyn Davies, Martin Brookes, and Neil Williams. "Technology, the Internet and the New Global Economy." Goldman Sachs Global Economics Paper No. 39, March 17, 2000.

of Goldman Sachs. The gains expected depend on the number and complexity of transactions along the supply chain. For that reason, it is doubtful that these numbers are meaningful for certain industries like forest products, where the table projects cost reductions associated with using IT of 15 to 25 percent even though the industry is relatively standardized. On the other hand, it would not be inappropriate to estimate a 10 to 15 percent saving on average across many industries operating in the U.S. economy.

The gains from e-business represent both cost reductions and improvements in convenience—goods should be not only cheaper but more readily available. Some of these gains come from the greatly reduced costs of distribution when consumers buy from the Web (B2C). So far, though, these gains have turned out to be small, perhaps because e-retailers do not handle the physical aspects of inventories and deliveries efficiently.

Large gains are likely in B2B supply chain management, as we noted earlier. These are the result of savings on huge amounts of paperwork and human interactions that have been very costly. Operating the supply chain automatically, perhaps even in real time, promises enormous savings in both costs and inventories. Ultimately these savings get passed on to consumers as lower product prices.

Unmeasured Gains

An important share—perhaps the most important—of the gains from IT and e-business is not measured. These are the gains to consumers in information and convenience in having access to the Internet. The volume of information at the user's fingertips is incredible, so extensive that some people are beginning to complain of an information overload. No matter where a user is in the world, an Internet connection provides entree to the world's most sophisticated libraries and news services.

Communication has become not only instantaneous but largely free. The computer user can look up products and order on the Web instead of going into a store. Admittedly, a search effort is required that might otherwise be done by a helpful sales person (though some Web sites will even search automatically to find where the product can be obtained at the lowest price). From the perspective of only five years ago, the saving in time and the gain in convenience are astonishing. The range of products, the flow of data, the geographic scope provide benefits that are not measured and indeed may not be measurable.

E-business and the technology on which it is based continue to make rapid progress, to the point that we do not yet know the full range of products and services that will become available electronically.

MACROECONOMIC EFFECTS

To evaluate the macroeconomic effects of the IT revolution, it is important to distinguish between short-run cyclical factors and long-run outcomes. In Chapter 2, we observed that the statistics about macroeconomic effects are so far uncertain. This reflects the fact that the period of increased aggregate productivity, 1996-2000, has been short. It is undeniable, however, that the IT revolution was a tremendous stimulus to the booming American economy in the late 1990s and that in turn its difficulties were largely responsible for the 2001 recession.

A number of studies have been carried out to evaluate the impact of IT on the U.S economy, though doing so is a challenge even for the most detailed computer models. Everything depends on the underlying assumptions about the nature and effects of technical and organizational change.

How can such a study be carried out? One approach is to begin on the micro level by studying developments sector by sector, as in Table 12.2. What are the effects of IT innovations on productivity or labor requirements? What are the effects on wages and prices? What are the effects on costs in the auto industry, banking, hotel services, airlines, and so on (see Table 12.2)? Tough questions to answer!

One calculation, based on work by the Council of Economic Advisers, deals directly with labor productivity. Table 12.3 shows labor productivity without adjustment for cyclical conditions or capital intensity. For each sector, the growth of labor productivity in the more recent period (1995-2000) is compared with the corresponding figure for the preceding six years (1989-1995).

The sectors vary greatly in productivity gains. Some, like durables manufacturing, show striking increases in both periods, perhaps reflecting expansion of production to meet high levels of demand; others, like construction, show declines in both periods. Communication actually shows a decline from its rapid productivity growth during 1989-1995 period, perhaps related to the staffing required to implement the drastic changes occurring in this sector with the introduction of fiberoptic lines and broadband connections.

Table 12.3: Labor Productivity in U. S. Industries

(Gross Domestic Income per Full Time Equivalent Employee, Annual Percent Changes)

	1989-1995	1995-2000	Difference
Agriculture	0.34	2.75	2.41
Mining	4.56	-1.78	-6.34
Construction	-0.10	-0.66	-0.56
Manufacturing	3.18	4.45	1.16
Durables	4.34	6.77	2.43
Non-durables	1.65	1.43	-0.23
Transportation	2.48	1.52	-0.96
Communication	5.07	2.19	-2.88
Electric/Gas/Sanitary	2.51	2.25	-0.26
Wholesale Trade	2.84	5.90	3.06
Retail Trade	0.68	4.74	4.05
Fire	1.70	3.51	1.81
Finance	3.18	9.53	6.34
Insurance	-0.28	0.42	0.70
Real Estate	1.38	2.80	1.42
Services	-1.12	0.08	1.21
Personal Services	-1.47	0.66	2.13
Business Services	-0.16	1.12	1.28
Health Services	-2.31	-0.23	2.09
Other Services	-0.72	-0.24	0.47

Source: M. N. Baily (2002). "The New Economy: Post Mortem or Second Wind?" Paper prepared for the meetings of the American Economic Association, Atlanta, January 4-6, 2002. (Based on data from the Bureau of Economic Analysis).

Wholesale and retail trade both show massive improvements, as does the finance category, which includes banking. These are sectors where electronic network connections have potential for substantial productivity improvements. Not surprisingly, services show less improvement, but the declines recorded for health services must reflect difficulties in measuring the performance of this sector, where there have certainly been technical advances and improvements in cure rates for many diseases.

A rough measure of the aggregate effect can be found using just a weighted average of the sector estimates (Table 12.4). The faster pace of productivity growth in the 1995-2000 period probably reflects new technologies and the emergence of e-business though, as we noted earlier, an upswing in the business cycle may also have had an influence.

Table 12.4: Aggregate Data on Labor Productivity

	1989-1995	**1995-2000**	**Difference**
Total Private Industries	0.88	1.97	1.09
IT-Intensive Half	2.43	4.15	1.72
Non-IT Intensive Half	-0.10	1.05	1.15

Sources: Martin Brookes and Z. Wahhaj. "The Shocking Economic Effect of B2B." Goldman Sachs Global Economics Paper No. 37, February 3, 2000; and Gavyn Davies, Martin Brookes, and Neil Williams. "Technology, the Internet and the New Global Economy." Goldman Sachs Global Economics Paper No. 39, March 17, 2000.
Note: Figures do not add up because of weighting.

The changes in productivity trends can be related to the IT intensity of the sectors: On average, sectors most heavily invested in IT show rapid growth in the 1989-95 period—an annual improvement averaging 1.75 percent between 1995 and 2000—while less IT-intensive sectors show no growth between 1989 and 1995 and an annual average improvement of only 1.15 percent from 1995 through 2000. That improvement may simply reflect the spillover of new technologies into the old economy. Overall, for all private industries, Table 12.4 suggests that there has been an annual improvement of approximately 1 percent, a figure not far from the data shown in Table 2.1.

A more typical approach is to look at the aggregate, making use of the growth accounting formulation based on inputs of capital and labor and the unexplained part of output growth, TFP, discussed in Chapters 2 and 11. Table 2.1 was a comparison of the results of a number of recent studies that used variants of this approach. These studies suggested that in the 1995-2000 period productivity, measured as output per hour, had speeded up from about 1.4 percent a year to about 2.5 percent. This has allowed aggregate output to grow more rapidly, by as much as 4.0 percent per year—substantially beyond its presumed non-inflationary ceiling of 2.5 percent.

While this represents a distinct improvement in the TFP trend, there is disagreement about how much of the change represents improvement in the computer sector alone and how much has already influenced the old sectors of the economy. In view of the dot-com crash and the recession, there is no agreement on when the economy will recover and whether, when it does, the speeded-up trend of new economy productivity growth can be expected to resume.

A DIGITAL DIVIDE?

Many social scientists have raised the possibility of a digital divide. What do they mean?

They are referring to the gap between people who have opportunity for regular access to the Internet and people who have little or no opportunity to access the Internet. The benefits of the knowledge economy will be disproportionately distributed between those who can take advantage of them and those who, through lack of training, skill, or IT access remain behind in the old economy. Since wealth and computer accessibility are closely correlated, the digital divide can be a powerful engine for continuing or indeed increasing income inequality. It implies a growing rift between those who are computer-empowered and those who are not, a difference with important social and political consequences.

Such a divide can occur:

- Within a country, between the increasingly well-off intellectual elite and the urban and rural poor.

- Between advanced countries that have renewed growth as a result of IT and networks and the less developed economies that have not yet jumped on the high-tech bandwagon and whose populations have little if any access to the Internet.

Turning first to the domestic version of the digital divide, Figure 12.3 shows that more than half of high-income people have access to computers and the Internet, compared with only 10 to 15 percent of low-income people.

As we have noted, the introduction of computer-based operations is skill-biased toward workers with greater training and more acquired skills. In the past decade, employers have increasingly sought and paid high wages to workers with significant computer abilities. Entrepreneurial opportunities have been more widely available in connection with the Internet and computers and some have been highly profitable. Meanwhile, wages of unskilled workers lagged behind as demand for labor in manufacturing declined with the importation of manufactured goods and as the immigrant population without computer skills increased.

Figure 12.3: A Digital Divide?

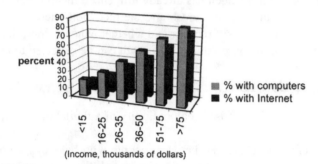

Computers and Internet access by household income, 2000

(Income, thousands of dollars)

- % with computers
- % with Internet

Source: World Bank Development Indicators Data.

The result has been a widening of income distribution. The rich get richer and the poor fall ever farther behind. The digital divide represents a serious social problem that calls for policy remedies.

Turning next to the international scene, Figure 12.4 shows the rift between the "have" and the "have not" countries.[11] Computer access in advanced countries like the United States, Canada, Australia, and South Korea is quite widespread. Western Europe and Japan are only a little behind, though we should note the rather different emphasis in these countries on cellular phones, where they are ahead of the United States, compared with Internet connections, where they are somewhat behind. (For Japan, see Case Study 12.4.)

Figure 12.4: A Digital Divide?
Between advanced and developing countries

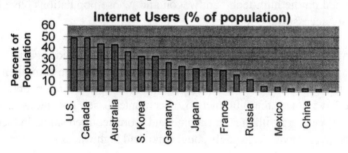

Internet Users (% of population)

Source: World Bank Development Indicators Data.

---

[11]Interesting comparisons for the OECD countries are provided in OECD (2001). *The New Economy: Beyond the Hype* (Paris: OECD); *<http://www.OECD.org/pdf/M00018622. pdf>*.

In many developing countries, computer use is still in its infancy, often because low-income people cannot afford expensive electronic equipment but also, and more significantly, because of a lack of electronic infrastructure, telephone lines, and Internet connections and the failure of the educational systems. There are, of course, striking exceptions, like the computer programming industry in Bangalore and the development of computer networks in Malaysia, but for many countries, entering the computer age will represent a policy challenge.

Case 12.3
The Internet in China

While the percentage of Internet penetration of the Chinese market is still very small in comparison with other East Asian countries (Figure 12.5, Panel A), the number of users is already very large (Figure 12.5, Panel B) The ultimate potential of the Chinese market of 1.3 billion people is tremendous. In recent years, China's networked computer activities are becoming the fastest-expanding market in Asia in absolute as well as relative terms. Despite the fact that computer applications in business are still underdeveloped today, China's e-business, like many other markets in China, represents a very attractive prospect as a result of its present underdevelopment and huge size.

China wants to move very rapidly to the other side of the digital divide. A number of factors favor rapid growth, but others present significant barriers. Among the relevant factors:

- Government policies have for some time favored building Internet infrastructure and use. Numerous "golden" projects sponsored by government departments have promoted e-activities, among them networks, debit cards, and applications like e-government. Still, government regulations remain murky. Important Internet sites and search engines (Google and Altavista) are often blocked for political reasons, though it is expected that rules permitting the entrance of foreign providers will be loosened in connection with China's membership in WTO.

- A number of backbone networks have been built, the largest by far of which, ChinaNet, is associated with the state-owned telecom companies. ChinaNet can in fact be said to have a semi-monopoly

Figure 12.5: China and the Internet

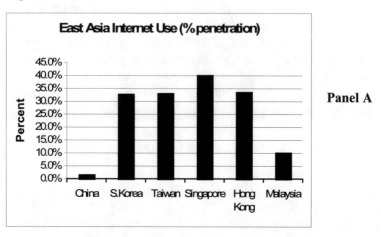

Panel A

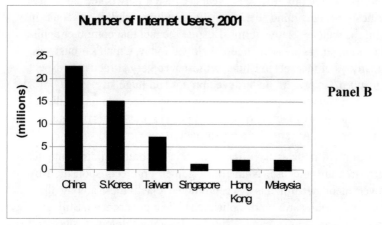

Panel B

Source: N. Zhao (2002). "Rapid Internet Development in China: A Discussion of Opportunities and Constraints on Future Growth." *Thunderbird International Business Review,* 44.(1): 119-38.

position.[12] Until recently, it was the only network to offer broadband service. Network speed generally appears to be slow until networks are upgraded.

- Telephone access to the Internet is much more readily available today than it was in the past, though much of telecom growth has been in cellular rather than wired service; but access remains rela-

---

[12]N. Zhao (2002). "Rapid Internet Development in China: A Discussion of Opportunities and Constraints on Future Growth." *Thunderbird International Business Review,* 44 (1): 119-38.

tively expensive. Zhao argues[13] that this is due to the high cost of line rental from ChinaNet, which is still the only legal way for the public to access the Internet.

- Personal computers are much less diffused than in neighboring countries, but China has become a builder of PCs and PC sales are forecast to expand rapidly. In mid-2001 approximately 10 million computers were connected to the Internet, of which 16 percent used leased lines and the rest dial-up systems. Since there are over 20 million users, each computer on average serves at least two users. The Internet café is very much a reality in China.

- In terms of sheer numbers, there are plenty of qualified personnel available in China, where engineering, including computer programming, accounts for a large percentage of college graduates. From the perspective of experience, however, the labor force is much more limited. China does have the latecomer advantage of being able to piggyback on programming systems already in use in more advanced countries.

- Internet connectivity and use in China are highly unequal, as is typical of the Chinese economy in general. Most Internet use is in the more advanced east and in the big cities.

- Internet use for commercial purposes must be adapted to Chinese commercial practice. A serious problem is that there is no national credit card system; most consumer e-business requires payment and pickup at the post office.

To summarize, it is almost certain that Internet use in China will continue to grow exponentially given the small market penetration of potential cell phone and Internet markets achieved so far. The number of future users is likely to be astronomical, making this a very attractive market for foreign and joint venture firms.

It is possible that China may seek to leapfrog its Internet development. One possible way to do this is through electronic banking services where e-payment could take the place of a check payment system. Another possibility is a leap toward wireless Internet access, as in Japan's I-mode. B2B activities may be the next area of interest because B2C commerce is still constrained by cultural factors and the lack of an efficient payment and delivery infrastructure.

---

[13]Ibid.

Case 12.4
E-Commerce in Japan: A Latecomer

Even though per capita income in Japan is almost as high as in the United States, Japan is far behind in Internet connections and e-commerce. Paradoxically, Japan is far ahead of the United States in wireless phones, many of which have some access to the Internet. These differences reflect cultural factors as well as significant differences in access.

In 2001 there were more than 100 million active Internet subscribers in the United States—almost 50 percent of the population; there were only 20 million active users in Japan—less than 20 percent of its population. The figures on e-business activity are probably even more disproportionate. Why?

The barriers to access are largely surmountable; their elimination is only a matter of time. The traditional PC takes a large amount of space, a problem in small Japanese apartments, but then the Japanese electronics industry has always been good at miniaturization. Fast Internet connections through the phone companies have been expensive and sometimes difficult to obtain, but that too can be fixed. Although applications like spreadsheets and databases are not being taught in most school programs, numerous private training schools have sprung up. The language of the Web is primarily English. Few Japanese feel comfortable with English and many are reluctant to do business in a foreign language. However, numerous Japanese language sites and portals have been created, some by foreign-based companies like Yahoo.

Cultural considerations are more difficult to deal with. Most Japanese "salarymen" stay at their place of work until all their tasks are done, so there is little professional need for a home computer. Japanese generally do not use checks to make payments; most transactions are in cash or by credit card. But the Japanese are reluctant to post their credit card numbers on a computer screen.

Most important is the fact that much business in Japan is built on personal relationships. Most people like to know the people they are doing business with and value their relationships with specific retailers and business associates. Many mistrust the impersonality of the Internet. Efforts are being made to overcome some of these barriers with, for example, portals that guarantee their merchants and delivery of orders through convenience stores. Still, many people express doubt that retail e-commerce will become widely popular in Japan.

On the other hand, cell phone use in Japan has been growing with astonishing speed. Cellular telephones are considered status symbols, particularly among the young. A growing number of these phones, DoCoMo's I-mode phones, have Internet access. The services and software products available over these wireless portals have been tailored to the needs and interests of their market—Games, street maps, news briefs, train schedules, weather reports, instant messaging, and, of course, e-mail are well-suited to the small screen on the cellular telephone. The wireless providers have set up a form of micro payment; charges for services are tacked onto the phone bill. For larger items it is possible to work with a local convenience store for delivery and payment.

It will be interesting to see how the Japanese and the American approaches to using the Internet will ultimately be reconciled.

Part IV
E-Business and the New Economy: The Future

Chapter 13

The Future of E-Business and the New Economy

"The term new economy *may be the best available description of changes taking place but is a dangerous term because it implies greater certainty about the future than actually exists."*[1]

"Prediction is difficult," the Danish physicist Niels Bohr is supposed to have said, "especially about the future." Predicting the future of e-business and the new economy is a special challenge.

Even though the dot-com bubble has burst, there is broad consensus that the information technology revolution is far from over. There are still enormous opportunities: Many applications are still in their infancy. Many are still far from market saturation. Indeed, the growing base of knowledge and the interactions between new ideas may allow the rate of innovation to accelerate in some fields. But not in all! Some applications are already approaching saturation in some countries or are reaching technical barriers to their rapid adoption.

While we can safely predict that there will be further rapid progress in general, it is much harder to specify where it will occur. Will bandwidth capacity and memory continue to increase as in the past? Will applications like e-books finally be accepted? How might the computer, the cell phone, and the personal digital assistant be combined? We have no idea what entirely new products will make the kind of splash in the future that so many have in the past decade.

To evaluate future potential, it is useful to distinguish between hardware and software and between various kinds of software e-business applications.

The technology underlying the basic hardware is still moving very rapidly. Though Moore's law has been operating for some 30 years, it is highly like-

---

[1]M. N. Baily (2002). "Macroeconomic Implications of the New Economy." Paper presented at the conference on Technology, Growth, and the Labor Market, Federal Reserve Bank of Atlanta, January 7.

ly that progress will continue at the same astonishing rate, with a doubling of the number of transistors on a chip every couple of years for at least another decade. The width of the microscopic circuit lines on a chip is still trending downward. Before long it will be less than one one-thousandth of the width of a human hair.

As transistor switches are reduced to atomic size and as the connecting wires get shorter and thinner, computer chips are becoming ever more complex and faster. They are consuming less electricity and generating less heat. This means that there will be more powerful computers in ever-smaller space. Similar rapid improvements are being made in glass-fiber communications and switching—one reason for the current surplus capacity in this field.

The power of the new equipment may be outrunning the needs of conventional users. Single-user programs for word processing or e-mail do not require, and often do not make good use of, super-fast new computers. On the other hand more powerful PCs expand the use of PCs into new areas. This was seen most recently with PCs capable of photo and video processing, tasks that required expensive specialized equipment until quite recently. There clearly will be further expansion in transmission capability, data storage, switching, and other equipment to support massive computation and broadband transmission.

How will these changes affect the hardware products that are available to consumers and business? The wearable or eyeglass computer is likely to remain little more than a gadget. An interesting discussion is whether consumers may want larger, more complex multipurpose computers or whether there will appear specialized consumer products like free-standing e-mail machines or word processors. Already most consumers use only a few of the functions available to them on their PCs. On the other hand, specialized single-function equipment has not so far been a commercial success, except for small portable units like PDAs and cellphones, and it is likely that these will be increasingly integrated. Simpler electronic circuits are going as controls into household equipment and motor vehicles. Wireless networks will allow increasing integration of computer equipment in the home and outside.

Consumer applications like word processing, data processing, digital photo handling, and electronic address and appointment calendars, which were all unknown some twenty or thirty years ago, have now reached a high degree of refinement. They are not likely to undergo radical change except for the addition or improvement of specific features like voice recognition.

The cost of massive computation and communication is likely to continue its rapid decline. Networks will continue to expand in size and complexity. This may change the operating mode of many computers so that they rely on programs in a central database rather than in the PC (that is the basis for

Microsoft's ".net" strategy). Electronic data communication protocols will become increasingly standardized, allowing the computer systems of many more enterprises to communicate directly with one another.

Integration is the watchword for both consumer and business software. In the past, many functions were carried out by separate programs that were often not well-suited to communicate with others, but increasingly programs are being integrated to communicate seamlessly.

Linking and integration of divergent computer systems and programs still has a long way to go. Many companies continue to use legacy systems that are incompatible with other systems even within the company, much less elsewhere. This is precisely why there are still many possibilities for improvements to enhance productivity, reduce labor costs, and facilitate customer service. But it will take many years and investment of much capital before integration is complete. Many of the gains of the new economy are still to come, awaiting the transformation of old industry operations to become consistent with the technological potentials of the IT revolution.

IT progress carries important implications for changing business operation and organization. It is already affecting many underlying economic realities: Transaction and communication costs are dropping rapidly. Voice recognition may reduce the need for human intervention, sharply cutting labor costs in consumer relationship management (CRM). Consumers and business managers, who now have much broader access to information, can better compare prices from alternative suppliers.

Some observers equate the broadening of markets with improved market efficiency. Many e-based operations offer tremendous economies of scale, gains that will favor large companies, yet at the same time computer networks provide newcomers with channels for market entry. All these changes will greatly influence the organization of business, affecting the optimal scale of operation and the nature of competition.

Productivity gains will vary greatly. Much depends on whether it is possible to automate to take advantage of progress in information technology, the expansion of competition, and the possibilities for international specialization. Clearly, the structure of the economy is already changing, from hard goods to soft goods, from personal interactions to computerized operations, from domestic to international markets.

MACROECONOMIC PROSPECTS

What can be said about the future from a macroeconomic perspective? What are the implications of the e-business revolution for GDP, for productivity, for prices? The typical procedure is to rely on trend estimates to make projections. The calculations of the aggregate impacts of the IT economy that we presented in Chapters 2 and 12 are a basis for such estimates.

Jorgenson and his associates[2] project the trend rate of labor productivity growth at 2.24 percent per year—almost as high as in the five years from 1995 to 2000. This estimate embodies TFP growth of 0.66 percent per year, only a little lower than in those five years. But the range of alternative projections in this study is very wide, reflecting uncertainties about technological progress in IT and its applications. The difficulty is that the mid-range forecast assumes that semiconductor and computer prices will continue to decline rapidly and that the enthusiastic pace of investment in high technology will once more become robust once the recession is over.

A related concern is that the big productivity gains were in booming wholesale and retail trade and the soaring securities markets. There is no assurance about when these businesses will recover from recession and whether they will resume their rapid growth. "If these assumptions do not fall into place, it is entirely possible that productivity would grow over time by less than 2 percent."[3]

Nevertheless, most analysts appear to be fairly optimistic, believing that recent productivity trends will be maintained and that productivity will not slump to the rates recorded before 1995. Baily notes, for example:

"Despite different perceptions of the drivers of productivity, it seems that the literature . . . all concludes the productivity trend is likely to be in the range of 2 to 2 1/2 percent per year. That is a strong performance that will increase wages and living standards and allow potential GDP growth in the range of 2.8 to 3.3 percent per year. It is certainly enough to say that the new economy will get a second wind."[4]

But he also notes: "Even though I conclude that the new economy will get a second wind, this does not mean a return to the economic euphoria of the late 1990s."

A more sophisticated approach is to introduce the information into an econometric model that takes into account the complex interactions of the economy, among them interindustry flows, the operation of markets on prices

[2]Dale W. Jorgenson. Mun S. Ho, and Kevin J Stiroh (2001), "Projecting Productivity Growth: Lessons from the U.S. Growth Resurgence." Paper prepared at the conference on Technology, Growth, and the Labor Market, Federal Reserve Bank of Atlanta, January 7.
[3]Jeff Madrick. *New York Times,* January 24, 2002.
[4]Martin Neil Baily (2002). "Macroeconomic Implications of the New Economy." Paper presented at the conference on Technology, Growth, and the Labor Market, Federal Reserve Bank of Atlanta, January 7; <*http://www.iie.com/catalog/wp/2001/01-9.pdf*>.

and wages, the role of interest rates and finance, and the influence of foreign trade. This approach yields estimates of aggregate effects year by year well into the future.

In the short and medium run, one to three years out, such calculations are useful to signal the turning point of the recession and the resumption of economic growth. A recovery from recession will come when both the inventory cycle ends and equipment purchases resume. Though signs of an inventory turnaround were already apparent in 2002, recovery of equipment investment was not on the immediate horizon.

Most econometric model forecasting services, like DRI-WEFA,[5] forecast economic recovery in 2003 and then a gradual return to 3.5 percent real GDP growth. The critical uncertainty is whether the business cycle will turn out to be V-shaped, U-shaped, or L-shaped or even whether there will be a double dip. A V-shaped cycle would mean rapid turnaround and rapid recovery. A U-shaped cycle would mean prolonged recession and rapid recovery thereafter. (The DRI-WEFA forecast lies somewhere between these two categories.) An L-shaped cycle suggests an extended period of stagnation.

A double dip (one dip after the other, not on top of the other like an ice cream cone) was widely feared when confidence declined as the accounting irregularities of Enron, World Com, etc. were being revealed in mid-2002. In view of the difficulties in the high-tech capital goods sector, excess telecom capacity, and the financial problems of the dot-coms, it is not unlikely that the current recession will last somewhat longer than the inventory adjustment.

Nevertheless, the rapid progress of IT is producing many new opportunities. Scores of new applications are already in existence. We are hopeful that the renewal of rapid IT innovations will soon buoy the recovery, but the timing cannot be predicted. It is also not too optimistic to speculate that, once rapid gains in productivity again appear, they will permit a favorable inflation/full employment relationship. That would mean price stability even when the economy is close to full employment.

Long-run forecasts are even more difficult. It is harder, of course, to predict how new technology and systems will affect various sectors of the economy over the long term. Some of the new technologies and their potential applications may only be a glimmer in an entrepreneur's eye. Once appropriate assumptions are introduced into the econometric model, the implied long-term trends must be appraised. Often, it is wise to consider alternative possibilities. It is also necessary to think about policies that may affect the long-term growth of the economy.

The trend estimate of growth is similar to the straight lines shown in Figure 2.1. The important question is whether the U.S. economy can in the

---

[5] DRI-WEFA (2002). *The U.S. Economy: 25-Year Focus.* Eddystone, PA: Global Insight.

long run achieve continued GDP growth at more than its historical 2.5 percent. The consensus answer to this question is "Yes," but there is always much uncertainty about the future.

To deal with the uncertainties of the long-term future, DRI-WEFA provides a number of alternative 25-year forecasts—a trend forecast, an optimistic forecast, and a pessimistic forecast[6] (see Table 13.1) These show a range of growth in output from 2002 through 2027 from 3.5 percent per year for the optimistic forecast to 2.4 percent per year for the pessimistic; these estimates bracket the historical record of 3.1 percent per year.

The productivity statistics, output per man-hour, are more hopeful: The optimistic projection of 2.6 percent annually and the pessimistic figure of 2.0 percent are both somewhat above the 1976-2002 record of 1.7 percent. Prospects for inflation are also predicted to be somewhat better than previously, with optimistic inflation rates of 2.3 percent and pessimistic rates 3.5 percent, compared to the historic rate of 4.0 percent.

Table 13.1: U. S. Long Term Forecasts
(% per year)

	History 1976-2001	Trend 2002-2027	Optimistic 2002-2007	Pessimistic 2002-2007
Potential GDP	3.1%	3.0%	3.5%	2.4%
GDP (real)	3.3%	3.1%	3.6%	2.6%
Productivity	1.7%	2.4%	2.6%	2.0%
Inflation	4.0%	2.8%	2.3%	3.5%

Source: DRI-WEFA (2002). *The U.S. Economy: 25-Year Focus*. Eddystone, PA: Global Insight.

In Table 13.2, a growth accounting exercise breaks down the contribution of inputs and the nature of improvements in factor productivity. These projections suggest a decline in the contribution of labor and capital to growth. The slower growth of the labor force results from the aging of the population. On the other hand, the estimates show some improvement in TFP growth in the optimistic forecast.

---

[6]The trend projection is a baseline scenario, the mean of various possible paths. The optimistic projection is an upside scenario that assumes a smooth growth path with rapid changes in technology. "The pickup in productivity growth, particularly over the next decade, is largely due to robust growth in equipment spending and new technologies." (DRI-WEFA, op. cit., no. 18). The pessimistic projection is a downside scenario assuming somewhat slower improvement in technology.

Table 13.2: Contributions to Potential GDP Growth (% per year)

	History		Trend		Optimistic		Pessimistic	
	1979-1989	1989-1999	2001-2006	2007-2027	2001-2007	2007-2027	2001-2008	2007-2027
Contribution of Inputs								
Labor Force	1.1%	1.0%	0.8%	0.7%	0.9%	0.9%	0.7%	0.6%
Capital Stock	0.9%	1.4%	1.1%	1.3%	1.2%	1.4%	1.0%	1.1%
Energy	0.0%	0.1%	0.1%	0.2%	0.1%	0.2%	0.1%	0.1%
Government Infrastructure	0.0%	0.0%	0.1%	0.1%	0.1%	0.1%	0.1%	0.1%
Total Inputs	2.1%	2.5%	2.1%	2.1%	2.3%	2.5%	1.9%	1.9%
TFP Growth	1.1%	1.2%	1.4%	1.2%	1.5%	1.4%	1.1%	0.8%

Note: Figures refer to private non-residential output; they do not sum to a broader total GDP measure.
Source: DRI-WEFA (2002). *The U.S. Economy: 25-Year Focus.* Eddystone, PA: Global Insight.

Forecasts by Goldman Sachs in 2002[7] produced the following predictions:

- A positive supply shock reflecting improvement in technology will raise GDP by 5 percent in major economies.

- Most of the measurable impact will result from B2B, which will rise to $1,500 billion in the United States in 2004.

- There will be little long-run impact on inflation, but inflation will be substantially reduced during the transition period.

- Productivity growth will be boosted and, given low unemployment, the inflation rate may be lower than it otherwise would be.

- Effects at first will be mainly in the United States but will appear rapidly in other parts of the world.

- While productivity and GDP are likely to shift upward for some years, new economy growth will not be rapid in the long term beyond a transition period.

Other long-term forecasts reach somewhat similar moderately optimistic conclusions.

---

[7]Martin Brookes, and Z. Wahhaj (2002). "The Shocking Economic Effect of B2B." Goldman Sachs Global Economics. Paper No. 37, February 3, 2000; Gavyn Davies, Martin Brookes, and Neil Williams (2002). "Technology, the Internet and the New Global Economy." Global Economic Paper No. 39, March 17.

Finally, we turn from the United States to a broader world perspective. We have already noted the puzzling fact that in the late 1990s most other countries did not show the same acceleration of productivity growth that was observed in the United States. It is not clear whether this reflects a special U.S. advantage with regard to the new technologies—the United States did, after all, provide a unique setting for e-business activities. The combination of more education, an entrepreneurial culture, venture capital, and deregulation made it easy to build new businesses, particularly in high-tech clusters like Silicon Valley.

Since most countries do not measure their GDP the same way as the United States does—they do not adjust prices for product quality change— some of the difference may simply be a question of measurement. Certainly in industries like cellular communications Europe and Japan have led the way, and some smaller countries have put more of their resources into advancing the wired economy.

Eventually, IT-related progress will affect all countries, directly through the adoption of new technology and indirectly through changes in the pattern of world trade. Advanced communications are already helping to diffuse e-technology to countries far from the source. But, as we consider further below, a country cannot simply leapfrog into the 21st century.

What is the ultimate potential for an e-business economy?

Advanced Countries

In a global world economy, industrial production is likely to migrate away from the advanced countries to the developing world, hence the idea of the *post-industrial economy.* This is the type of society that will eventually prevail in the most advanced countries. Arguably, the United States, Singapore, and some advanced countries in Europe may already be approaching that point. It is a society where there is little physical manufacturing and most manufactured goods are imported. This type of society specializes in sophisticated services like finance, engineering, entertainment, and consulting. There is room here for extensive use of computers. High-value activities will capitalize on computation integrated with brain power—high-tech skills, education, and experience. That will tend to expand work opportunities and raise salaries of the computer-skilled relative to unskilled workers.

Though the notion of the *digital economy* sounds attractive, there is only so much that can be accomplished electronically. Still, IT can be helpful in many of the tasks of daily life and in many of the transactions that relate to them. There will be an enormous expansion of electronic networks and even of electronic decision making, though even the most advanced economy cannot be 100 percent automated and electronic: In the end, we must feed our children, wash the dishes, and mow the lawn. The post-industrial economy will have a heavy emphasis on service activities, some of which will be connected with sophisticated e-businesses but many of which will remain personal services

Case 13.1
The Work of Nations

Robert Reich[8] divides workers into three categories: knowledge workers (for want of a better word he calls them *symbolic analysts*), in-person service workers, and routine production workers.

Much knowledge work relates to managing and developing e-business, but much will also apply to high-level services like finance, law, engineering, and programming. Some will be concerned with providing content: writing scripts and acting in movies or composing advertising jingles. The skills required will be in short supply and knowledge workers will make increasingly high salaries.

In-person service workers like housekeepers, waiters, and retail store staff do not need high-level skills. Their salaries will depend greatly on supply and demand and may be held down by the flow of immigrants eager to take such jobs.

Routine production employment will decline in the advanced countries, shifting to the developing world as industry moves to low-wage countries.

Developing Countries

The IT revolution offers some important opportunities, but many of these countries also face some important barriers.

We note the diversity of the developing world: Some countries are already quite far up the development ladder. Taiwan, South Korea, and Malaysia have become the world's leading producers of high-tech electronic products—chips, PCs, screens, disk drives, and related equipment. South Korea is far advanced in providing cellular phone service. Singapore plans a wired economy.

As geographic distance diminishes in importance, other countries also may quickly join the IT revolution. In some countries like Israel, Russia, and parts of India, clusters of computer engineers are beginning to develop IT hardware and programming industries. Elsewhere, in many parts of Asia and Africa where there are still important barriers, the transition to a digital world will be challenging. E-technology and e-business, even e-government, are the watchwords of economic development planning in many countries.

---

[8]Robert Reich (1992). *The Work of Nations.* New York: Vintage Books.

But the barriers are gigantic. Telephonic infrastructure is inadequate, though cellular service has been introduced rapidly in many areas. Computer Internet access, especially broadband, is limited in the cities and may be totally unavailable in rural areas. Business culture still relies on personal interactions between buyers and sellers and transactions are still paid for in cash.

Inadequate education may continue to stand in the way of the IT revolution in developing countries. It takes many years, at least a generation, to significantly improve the quantity and quality of education. Technical training may be difficult to organize. The industrial development policies introduced by many countries to move the economy into the computer age may not be able to quickly overcome the challenges of complex modern technology.

That leaves *a global economy* where much of the highly paid sophisticated knowledge-based work is in the advanced countries (but not all—remember the programmers in Bangalore). Service and industrial workers will make some progress but their earnings will continue to be low relatively to more technically skilled employees. There will be broad differences between people who can take advantage of the computer and those who cannot.

That sounds very much like a continuation of the digital divide.

Concluding Comment: The Future

- On the firm level, reductions in transaction, communication, and transportation costs will have important effects on business operations and organization.

- Some industries, even in the old economy, will gain greatly depending on the impact of networking and new organizations.

- Increased internationalization will affect the structure of industry.

- There may be a digital divide both domestically and internationally.

- In the short-term, at the macro level, the potential of IT may help return the economy to prosperity. In the long run, there will continue to be gains in productivity.

Chapter 14

How to Participate in the New Economy

What can be done to participate in the new economy? We first discuss public policy. Then we consider the stakeholders and how they can participate in the new economy.

E-BUSINESS AND POLICY

The new economy poses significant new challenges from both a micro and a macro-economic perspective.

The micro issues relate to industrial organization, competition, encouragement of technical change, and innovation. The macro questions relate to maintaining growth, full employment, and price stability.

Micro Policy

There is little doubt about the aims of public policy on IT and e-commerce. Policy-makers everywhere are trying to advance their countries into the 21st century by promoting high-tech industry, communication, and e-commerce. This is widely thought to be the way of the future. But precisely how to formulate these policies and how they should fit in to a country's economic culture are far from clear.

A cultural and philosophical issue is whether technological progress can be best stimulated through the public sector or through private sector entrepreneurship. In the United States, public sector intervention and planning has been very limited. Though there was in the early 1990s an effort to create an information superhighway, even that was to be dominated largely by the private sector, though with encouragement and supervision from the public sector. Basic science received considerable government support and we are often reminded that the Internet started out as a project of a Defense Department unit, DARPA (Defense Advabced Research Projects Agency). Yet the rapid development of IT and of its applications in e-commerce in the United States was largely a phenomenon of the private sector. As we have noted, easing of government regulations and outright deregulation, the availability of venture capital, interaction between universities and business, and an entrepreneurial culture made a fertile setting for rapid changes in technology and business organization.

Many other countries have taken a similar approach, though their entrepreneurial tradition or financial environment may not be as suitable. In Japan, for example, the proportion of start-up IT companies is very much smaller than in the United States or Europe. This is probably a reflection of cultural and business organizational factors, especially the greater reliance in Japan on large businesses.

Some other countries have tried to follow a more directed route. While the tradition of government planning has faded worldwide, in some countries government action and public sector plans are being used to advance IT development. In Malaysia, Cyberjaya, the creation of a wired corridor, and encouragement for IT and e-business operations to locate there is an example. The proposal to make Singapore a wired island is another. In these cases, the public sector has defined a strategy of high-tech or e-business development, though implementation remains largely with the private sector.

This raises the old debate about the merits of selective industrial policies. The idea was to promote "sunrise" industries and to phase out "sunset" activities. Economists are still debating whether such policies help or hinder economic growth.[1] The effectiveness of such policies on high-tech IT industries, the Internet, and e-business may be quite different now than it was when basic materials industries and manufacturing were being built at an earlier stage of economic development. Broad government support may be helpful to e-business development only if it promotes entrepreneurial experimentation and competition.

In Chapter 11 we discussed some of the contradictory competitive forces that arise out of the e-business revolution. On the one hand, rapid technological change has stimulated competition, Schumpeter style, as new businesses replace the old. On the other hand, we have seen a number of ways in which dominant players can establish and maintain a monopoly position. We have noted the advantages of first movers and of firms that set the industry standard. We are aware of the effects of enormous economies of scale. Though the initial cost of many developments is high, the cost of their proliferation is minimal, so large-scale operations are favored. There are also numerous opportunities for bundling or tying, linking the sale of one product to the purchase of another in which the seller may already have a dominant position. What should be public policy under these circumstances?

---

[1]World Bank (1993). *The East Asian Miracle.* New York: Oxford.

The Microsoft case illustrates the difficulties of establishing appropriate policies. In a complex entrepreneurial world, it is important to minimize intervention and regulation. Moreover, it is important to provide patent protection and to insure that copyrights cannot be violated willy-nilly. Today's antitrust and intellectual property protection laws are not well-adapted to deal with these situations. There may be trade-offs between allowing firms to maintain monopoly power and the rate of technical change.

Yet though large dominant firms devote huge resources to research and development, it is not clear that they will make the big leap from current systems, perhaps tweaked by new features, to the revolutionary advanced model. That is why there is significant disagreement between those who promote open systems competition to stimulate technical change and those who see progress in stable well-managed proprietary systems.

There is widespread agreement, however, that policy should foster technological change and competition. This will mean policies to stimulate education and computer access, venture capital financing, and help to start-up firms. Different patent and copyright protections may be part of the required policy mix. What type of antitrust enforcement is appropriate is unfortunately still wide open.

Macro Policy

The macro policy challenges are illustrated by those encountered in the United States by the Greenspan-directed Federal Reserve in the late 1990s. As we have described, the Federal Reserve went a long way toward recognizing the new economy, resisting pressure to apply policy brakes before the economy reached its capacity ceiling. But the difficulty was that irrational exuberance allowed the boom to go on too long and stock markets to go too high; the result was a crash. Other countries may face similar or perhaps even more difficult problems because they are more exposed to foreign exchange market fluctuations than the United States.

Maintaining economic stability is exceedingly important to achieving economic development. The speculative aspects of the e-business/high-tech world, where dreams sometimes exceed accomplishment, make the task much more difficult.

Today's problem, in the United States and in many other countries, is how to stimulate economic activity. When that is accomplished, hopefully government officials will be able to control the expansion and avoid extreme fluctuations in the business cycle—because it has become quite clear that the business cycle is very much a part of the new economy.

Longer term, a major element of policy is to stimulate growth. In the United States, government funding has gone largely to basic research, where it has been important. With some exceptions, however, actual applications have been created by private businesses, large and small, seeking to enhance their market position and their profits. This pattern is likely to continue in the U.S. Other countries that have traditionally had more proactive growth and development policies are now turning their policy tools to advancing the digital economy. That may involve such policy elements as support for advanced education, building wired and wireless Internet infrastructure, tax incentives for R&D, and promotion of foreign investment.

HOW CAN STAKEHOLDERS PARTICIPATE?

Who are the stakeholders? How can they participate in the new economy?

Consumer stakeholders must be equipped to make maximum use of the Internet. Most important, that calls for familiarity with the basics of computer techniques. They must learn how to run their e-mail, how to search for information on the World Wide Web, and how to communicate with some of the basic programs available. Paradoxically, since computer programs are supposed to have simple and intuitive interfaces, except for the computer specialist, a high level of computer sophistication is *not* required.

Worker stakeholders must be prepared to work in a computerized economy, to learn new programs and new technologies. That may require life-long education. Some experts will need to achieve high levels of technical skill to deal with complex computer algorithms and to build the complex new systems that will integrate an Internet-based business world. Other workers, who will exercise more practical skills like data input, may need only to be familiar with the standard programs.

Entrepreneur stakeholders must ask whether e-business offers opportunities for their firms—whether the investment in computers, programming, and management is worthwhile. That depends greatly on the nature of the business. Retail vending sites or small shops are easy to set up on the Web, but complicated catalog sites may be costly to start up and operate. Entrepreneurs must keep in mind that for physical goods the tasks of delivery and returns must be handled in conventional ways.

Above all, these stakeholders need a realistic, achievable business and financial plan, one that will produce revenue and profits before the venture capital runs out. The more complex the business, the wiser it is to hire professional advice in putting into place an e-business strategy.

As *investors,* stakeholders must learn to evaluate both the profit potential and the risks of new e-business ventures. This is a special challenge if the investor wants to participate in innovative projects where technology and competition are far different from those to be met with in conventional bricks-and-mortar enterprises. It is easy to be "blown away" by the euphoria associated with a visionary new project.

Economic policy makers are interested in promoting the country's participation in the new economy. This is a major challenge in many countries because it calls for an educated and technically sophisticated labor force. The United States had a unique advantage—an already high level of technology, a spirit of enterprise, and considerable amounts of venture capital looking for investments. These came together to create Silicon Valley and similar high-tech clusters elsewhere. Few other countries have the same mixture. Some that have high levels of computer skills lack an entrepreneurial tradition. Many countries lack the education and the physical infrastructure that the e-conomy requires.

A country need not be the developer of the new technology in order to use it. Indeed, as we have noted, the advantage of countries that are only now joining the electronic world is that they can profit from the knowledge and experience that other countries have already acquired. To participate in the growth of the new economy, however, most countries will be well advised to promote education, computer literacy, and Internet connections as well as drawing as much as possible on the vast store of knowledge that has already been accumulated.

IS THERE A NEW ECONOMY?

The future is only a matter of time! Where economic and technological progress is concerned, that statement is not quite as simplistic as it sounds. As we have noted, the acquisition of knowledge is linear. New ideas and inventions progress one after the other; what has been learned becomes the basis for further development.

In recent years the pace of invention and innovation has accelerated. We are in the middle of a revolution. The introduction of computers and networking has made it possible to replace many functions that depended on human action with automatic or semi-automatic computerized procedures.

In 1895, officials of the U.S. Patent Bureau announced that all significant inventions had already been made. With equal certainty, and I hope with greater accuracy, we can predict that there will be many more new developments over the coming decades. The potential for innovations in the operations of business is far from exhausted. Indeed, many of the products and procedures that have recently emerged are not yet widely diffused even in the most advanced countries. And the developing countries still have a long way to go to catch up. Inevitably, new business processes based on the IT/e-business revolution will continue to be introduced. We cannot be certain how fast, but we can be certain that in the absence of catastrophe or resource constraints, further progress will be made.

The question we have posed is whether this wave of technological progress will result in a new economy. So far the statistical evidence is still equivocal. We cannot be certain that the changes we have seen—improvements in productivity, easing of inflationary pressures—reflect a new economy or simply a temporary phase of the old one. It is quite possible, after all, that improvements in productivity will continue for a time as the economy adjusts to the introduction of new computer-assisted ways of operation.

Whether there is a new economy or not depends on how we are defining our terms:

- If we define the new economy in terms of measured aggregate economic performance—higher productivity growth, lower inflation, no business cycle—our answer has to be equivocal: "No, Virginia, we cannot be sure there is a new economy."

- If we define the new economy as a wave of innovations—new products and services, substitution of automatic systems for human interaction, a dynamic economy—our answer is strongly positive: "Yes, Virginia, there is a new economy!"

Bibliography

Baily, M. N. (2002a). "The New Economy: Post Mortem or Second Wind." Paper presented at the American Economics Association meetings, Atlanta, January 4-6, 2002.

Baily, M. N. (2002b). "Macroeconomic Implications of the New Economy." Paper presented at the conference on "Technology, Growth, and the Labor Market," Federal Reserve Bank of Atlanta, January 7, 2002.

Baily, M. N., and Robert Lawrence (2001). "Do We Have a New Economy?" *American Economic Review: Papers and Proceedings,* 91 (2): 308-12.

Bresnahan, Timothy F., E. Brynjolfsson, and L. M. Hitt (2002). "Information Technology, Workplace Organization, and the Demand for Skilled Labor: Firm-level Evidence." *Quarterly Journal of Economics,* 117: 339-76; *<http://ebusiness.mit.edu/erik>*.

BRIE-IGCC E-conomy Project (2001). *Tracking a Transformation: E-Commerce and the Terms of Competition in Industries.* Washington: Brookings Institution Press.

Brookes, Martin, and Z. Wahhaj (2000). "The Shocking Economic Effect of B2B." Goldman Sachs Global Economics Paper No. 37.

Brynjolfsson, Erik, and Lorin M. Hitt (2000). "Beyond Computation: Information Technology, Organizational Transformation, and Business Performance." *Journal of Economic Perspectives,* 14 (4): 23-48; *<http://ebusiness.mit.edu/erik>*.

Brynjolfsson, Erik, and S. Yang (1997). "The Intangible Costs and Benefits of Computer Investments: Evidence from Financial Markets." *Proceedings of the International Conference on Information Systems,* Atlanta; *<http://ebusiness.mit.edu/erik>*.

Chandler, Alfred D. (1977). *The Visible Hand.* Cambridge, MA: Harvard University Press.

Christenson, Clayton M. (2000). *The Innovator's Dilemma.* New York: Harper Business.

171

Coase, Ronald (1937). "The Nature of the Firm." *Economica,* 4: 386-405.

Council of Economic Advisers (2000, 2001, and 2002). *Economic Report of the President.* Washington: Government Printing Office.

Davies, Gavyn, Martin Brookes, and Neil Williams (2000). "Technology, the Internet and the New Global Economy." Goldman Sachs Global Economic Paper No. 39.

David, Paul (1990). "The Dynamo and the Computer: An Historical Perspective on the Modern Productivity Paradox." *American Economic Review Papers and Proceedings,* 1990: 355-60.

Denison, Edward F. (1974). *Accounting for U.S. Economic Growth.* Washington: Brookings Institution Press.

DRI-WEFA (2002). *The U.S. Economy; 25-Year Focus.* Eddystone, PA: Global Insight.

Encyclopedia of the New Economy. Lycos; *<http://hotwired.lycos.com/special/ene>.*

Federal Reserve Bank of Dallas (200l). *Southwest Economy.*

Florian, E. (2001). "Dead and (Mostly) Gone Dot-coms." *Fortune,* December 24, 2001.

Gordon, Robert J. (2000). "Does the New Economy Measure up to the Great Inventions of the Past?" *Journal of Economic Perspectives,* 4 (14): 40-74.

Greenspan, Alan (1999). "New Challenges for Monetary Policy." *<http://www .federalreserve.gov/boarddocs/speeches/speeches/1999/19990827.htm>.*

Hunter, Larry W., A. Bernhardt, K., L. Hughes, and E. Skuratowicz (2000). "It's Not Just the ATMs: Firm Strategies, Work Restructuring and Workers' Earnings in Retail Banking." Unpublished. Philadelphia: Wharton School.

IMF (International Monetary Fund) (2001). *World Economic Outlook: The Information Technology Revolution.* Washington: IMF.

Jorgenson, Dale W. (2001). "Information Technology and the U.S. Economy." *American Economic Review,* 94 (1): 1-32.

Jorgenson, Dale W., Mun Ho, and Kevin J. Stiroh (2001). "Projecting Productivity Growth: Lessons from the U.S. Growth Resurgence." Paper prepared for the conference on "Technology, Growth, and the Labor Market." Federal Reserve Bank of Atlanta, January 7, 2001.

Kahn, J. A., and M. M. McConnell (2002). "Has Inventory Volatility Returned? A Look at the Current Cycle." *Current Issues in Economics and Finance,* 8 (5): 1-6, Federal Reserve Bank of New York.

Kamarainen, V., J. Smaros, T. Jaakola, and J. Holstrom (2001). "Cost Effectiveness in the E-Grocery Business." *International Journal of Retail and Distribution Management,* 29 (1); *<http://www.diem.hut.fi/ecomlog>.*

Knowledge@Wharton (3/19/01). "New Economy or Old Economy: A Shakeout is a Shakeout." *<http://knowledge.wharton.upenn.edu/articles.cfm?catid=4&articleid=318>.*

Knowledge@Wharton (4/20/01). "Will Covisint Thrive as a B2B Exchange?" *<http://knowledge.wharton.upenn.edu/articles.cfm?catid=14&articleid=353>.*

Knowledge@Wharton (11/21/01). "The Evolution of B2B: Lessons from the Auto Industry." *<http://knowledge.wharton.upenn.edu/articles.cfm?catid=14&articleid=466>.*

Kindleberger, Charles P. (1996). *Manias, Panics, and Crashes: A History of Financial Crises,* 3rd ed. New York: Wiley.

Krugman, Paul (2000). "Can America Stay on Top?" *Journal of Economic Perspectives,* 14 (1): 172, pp. 168-176.

Kuhn, Thomas S. (1962). *The Structure of Scientific Revolutions.* Chicago: University of Chicago Press.

Kwoka, John E. (2001). "Automobiles: The Old Economy Collides with the New." *Journal of Industrial Organization,* 19: 55-69.

Lau, Lawrence, J. (2000). "The New Chinese Economy: A View from the Outside." *<http:www,stabdfird,edy/~ljlau>.*

Leibowita, Stan (2002). *Re-Thinking the Networked Economy.* New York: Amacom Press.

Levy, Frank, A. Beamish, R. J. Murnane, and D. Autor (2000). "Computerization and Skills: Examples from a Car Dealership." Unpublished. MIT.

Murnane, Richard J., F. Levy, and D. Autor (1999). "Technological Change, Computers and Skill Demands: Evidence from Back Office Operations of a Large Bank." Cambridge: NBER Labor Workshop.

Nelson, Richard R., and S. G. Winter (1982). *An Evolutionary Theory of Economic Change.* Cambridge, MA: Harvard University Press.

OECD (Organization for Economic Cooperation and Development) (2001). *The New Economy: Beyond the Hype.* Paris: OECD; *<http://www.OECD.org/pdf/M00018000/M00018622.pdf>.*

Oliner, Stephen D., and Daniel E. Sichel (2000). "The Resurgence of Growth in the Late 1990s: Is Information Technology the Story?" *Journal of Economic Perspectives,* 14 (4): 3-32.

Reich, Robert B. (2002). *The Future of Success.* New York: Random House, Vintage Books.

Reich, Robert B. (1992). *The Work of Nations.* New York: Vintage Books.

Robles, Fernando (2002). "The Evolution of Global Portal Strategy." *Thunderbird International Business Review,* 1: 25-47.

Romer, Paul (1986). "Increasing Returns and Long-Run Growth." *Journal of Political Economy,* 94: 1002-37.

Schumpeter, Joseph A. (1945, 1975). *Capitalism, Socialism, and Democracy.* New York: Harper.

Solow, Robert M. (1957). "Technical Change and the Aggregate Production Function." *Review of Economics and Statistics,* 39: 312-20.

Solow, Robert M. (1989). *Growth Theory: An Exposition.* New York: Oxford University Press.

Solow, Robert M. (1987). *New York Times* Book Review, July 12, 1987, p. 36.

Stiroh, Kevin J. (2001). "Projecting Productivity Growth: Lessons from the U.S. Growth Resurgence." Paper prepared for the conference on "Technology, Growth, and the Labor Market." Federal Reserve Bank of Atlanta, January 7.

Tripplet, Jack E. (1999). "The Solow Productivity Paradox: What Do Computers Do to Productivity?" *Canadian Journal of Economics,* 32 (2): 309-34.

U. S. News and World Report (2001). "Special Report: E-Learning." October 15, 2001; *<http://www.usnews.com/usnews/edu/elearning/articles/right.htm>*.

University of Texas (undated). "The Internet Economy Indicators," study sponsored by Cisco.

World Bank (1993). *The East Asian Miracle.* New York: Oxford University Press.

Yang, Shinkyu, and E. Brynjolfsson (2001). "Intangible Assets and Growth Accounting." Research Paper, MIT; *<http://ebusiness.mit.edu/erik>; <http://www.internetindicators.com/indicators.html>*.

Zhao, N. (2002). "Rapid Internet Development in China: A Discussion of Opportunities and Constraints on Future Growth." *Thunderbird International Business Review,* 44 (1): 119-38.

Index

1-800-Flowers.com, 53

A

Abrahams, P., 63
Advanced countries, 162
Advantages of e-business for firms, 138
   See also Economics of e-business, The;
   Economic impact of e-business.
Ahao, N., 148
Amazon.com, 47, 53
American Economic Review, 23, 24, 25
An alphabet soup of IT businesses and
   experiences, 75

B

B2B, 4, 47
   See also Business-to-business.
B2B exchanges, 73-76
   Covisint, 74
   See also E-business revolution, The; E-
   Commerce: Supply chain management.
B2C, 4, 47-48
   See also Business-to-consumer; E-com-
   merce: B2C.
Baily, M. N., 155
Baker, T., 63
BarnesandNoble.com, 53
Bell Labs, 9
Brookes, Martin, 161
Browning, John, 6

Brynjolfsson, Erik, 26, 27, 111, 135
Business practice and organization,
   130-132
   See also Economics of e-business, The;
   Economic impact of e-business.
Business-to-business, 4
   See also B2B
Business-to-consumer, 4
   See also B2C
Business Week, 6, 7

C

Canadian Journal of Economics, 22
Chadwicks.com, 53
Chandler, Alfred D., 114
Changes in business practice and
   organization, 38-39
   See also Technological/organization
   revolution; New economy and the dot-
   com crash, The.
Christenson, Clayton M., 50
CIO Magazine, 72
Cisco, 71, 72
Cisco Systems, 71-73
   See also E-business revolution, The;
   E-commerce: Supply chain management.
Coase, Ronald, 113